The Coming of Our God

Scriptural Reflections
for
Advent, Christmas and Epiphany

Patrick J. Ryan, S.J.

Illustrations by
Charlotte Lichtblau

Paulist Press
New York/Mahwah, N.J.

Cover design by Cynthia Dunne

Interior illustrations by Charlotte Lichtblau

Library of Congress Cataloging-in-Publication Data

Ryan, Patrick J., 1939–
    The coming of our God : scriptural reflections for Advent, Christmas, and Epiphany / Patrick J. Ryan.
        p.   cm.
    ISBN 0-8091-3880-8 (alk. paper)
    1. Advent Meditations.   2. Christmas Meditations.   3. Epiphany season Meditations.   4. Bible Meditations.   5. Catholic Church Prayer–books and devotions–English.   I. Title.
BX2170.A4R83   1999
242´.33–dc21   99-30275
                                                                                    CIP

Published by Paulist Press
997 Macarthur Boulevard
Mahwah, New Jersey 07430

www.paulistpress.com

Printed and bound in the
United States of America

*"Carry me along, taddy, like you done
through the toy fair!"*

–James Joyce, *Finnegans Wake*

Introduction

The coming of our God
To fill our world with peace
Should make us raise our voices high
In songs that never cease.

Hymn by Charles Coffin, 1736

The seasons of Advent, Christmas and Epiphany all cele-brate one startling event: the coming of our God into human history. The English names for these seasons derive respec-tively from Latin *(adventus)*, Old English *(Cristes Maesse)* and Greek *(epiphaneia)*. The first and the third turn out to be dif-ferent ways of expressing what theology (following Jn 1:14) calls the incarnation, the enfleshment of God in Jesus, imaged spatially as his coming or arrival (Advent) or visually as his appearance or manifestation (Epiphany). Old English and its descendants concentrate, in the naming of the second sea-son, on the eucharistic celebration of that mystery, "Christ's Mass." Other European languages, such as Italian, call Christmas the birthday *(Natale)* of Jesus or, as in French, the Good News about his birth *(Noël,* related to *nouvelles)* first announced to shepherds by an angelic host (Lk 2:10).

The celebration of the incarnation began later in church

history than the celebration of the Christian Passover memorializing the death and resurrection of Jesus, his passing through dark waters into the glorious homeland of God. Somewhat in imitation of the paschal seasons of Lent and Easter, the Advent-Christmas-Epiphany cycle began to develop in Gaul in the fourth century A.D. as a preparation for baptism at the liturgical celebration of the baptism of Jesus. The Roman Christian need to compete with the popular pagan celebration (somewhat Eastern and Mithraic in its origins) of the rebirth of the Unconquered Sun *(Sol Invictus)* on December 25, an innovation the Emperor Aurelian inaugurated in A.D. 274, may have led to the location of the feast of the newborn "Sun of Righteousness" *(Sol Justitiae)* just after the winter solstice.

Advent today is defined as the season preceding the solemnity of the Birth of Our Lord, including at least four Sundays beginning from the Sunday closest to the feast of Saint Andrew the Apostle (November 30). The Christmas season stretches from the vigil of Christmas (the evening of December 24) to the eve of the solemnity of the Epiphany, January 6 where it is a public holiday or, as in the United States, the second Sunday after Christmas. Epiphany includes all the days from the solemnity of the Epiphany to the feast of the Baptism of the Lord (the third Sunday after Christmas or the day after Epiphany Sunday if Epiphany occurs on a Sunday as late as January 7 or 8).

From my earliest days as a Jesuit I have loved the Advent-Christmas-Epiphany cycle. Those who knew me as a novice will recall the Jesse tree I helped to create at Bellarmine College in Plattsburgh, New York, and the mimeographed booklet of readings I composed to accompany it. My love for this time of the church year has increased with the reform of the Catholic lectionary in 1969 and the specification of liturgical readings not only for three cycles of Sundays and some major feasts but also for the weekdays of these seasons. To facilitate reading this book with an American lectionary, I have used the 1986 edition of the New American Bible for all biblical quotations–the same translation used in the lectionary.

Between 1987 and 1993 I contributed the columns entitled "The Word" in *America,* the American and Canadian Jesuit journal of opinion. Some of the Sunday and solemnity reflections in this book derive from those columns, but all are considerably revised or even completely rewritten. I have also written reflections on the lectionary readings for the weekdays of this cycle for this publication. The drawings by Charlotte Lichtblau that appear in this volume originally accompanied the columns that appeared in *America.* I am grateful to her and to the editors of *America* for their permission to reproduce these drawings in this volume.

The reflections are not meant as a collection of homilies but as a series of meditations, longer or shorter, to accompany those who make this journey through the darkest days of the year into the light of Christ "manifested in the flesh,/ vindicated in the spirit;/ seen by angels,/ proclaimed to the Gentiles,/ believed in throughout the world,/ taken up in glory" (1 Tm 3:16). My own meditations spring from the imagination of a historian of religion who has spent half of his years as a Jesuit in multicultural settings outside the United States, mainly in Africa. But even in New York, my native city, I find myself more and more living in a cross-cultural, multireligious situation–as do we all. Advent, Christmas and Epiphany speak to me in this setting. Perhaps they will speak to you as well.

The
First
Week
of
Advent

"...The daybreak from on high will visit us...." (Lk 1:78)

First Sunday of Advent (A)

Readings: Isaiah 2:1–5; Romans 13:11–14;
Matthew 24:37–44

Cataclysms

Disasters fascinate us: the sinking of the *Titanic*, the *Lusitania* and the *Andrea Doria*; the volcanic eruption of Mount Vesuvius, the Great Fire of London and the Lisbon earthquake; the Black Plague of the fourteenth century, the influenza epidemic of the early twentieth century and the AIDS crisis of recent times. Suitably or unsuitably, each disaster serves us as a model for the next. "Human kind cannot bear very much reality," T. S. Eliot wrote. The newness of every historical phenomenon appalls us and we look for parallels in the past, as if to assure ourselves that we have survived as bad or worse and we will surely survive again.

Trying to face up to the disaster that was the destruction

of the Temple in Jerusalem in A.D. 70, the Jews and Christians of that era compared it to the Chaldean devastation of Jerusalem in 587 B.C. or the profanation of the Temple by Antiochus IV Epiphanes in 167 B.C. But the Roman devastation of Jerusalem and its newly completed Temple proved to have much more lasting effects. Today, more than five decades after the restoration of Jewish sovereignty in modern Israel, Israeli society would face an internal crisis of monumental proportions if its Orthodox Jewish population should press for a restoration of sacrificial worship in the Temple.

Expectation of the end of times and the triumphant rule of Jerusalem over the rest of the known world had reached a fever pitch in some Palestinian Jewish circles by the first century A.D. Greek cultural imperialism and Roman military oppression had driven the historically blocked Jewish nation to desperate thoughts. Jesus had to differentiate himself from other claimants to the title of *messiah,* anointed ruler of the future and glorious Jewish kingdom. After the time of Jesus, when the Zealot movement had provoked a disastrous conflict with the Romans (A.D. 66–70), the gospel writers took pains as well to differentiate the messianic status of Jesus from something that might have interested the Zealots. Toward the end of the New Testament era, the Roman emperor Hadrian had dispersed the Jews from Jerusalem and renamed it Aelia Capitolina. The life of any Jew claiming messianic status and political independence for the Jewish people was forfeit.

These developments in the late first century and the early second century A.D. color Matthew's presentation of the eschatological discourse of Jesus. Unlike political messiahs, Matthew's Jesus insisted on the mysteriousness of "the coming of the Son of Man" (Mt 24:37). The coming of that perfect human being of whom Daniel wrote (Dn 7:13–14) would not be so obvious as in Daniel's vision. Popular eschatological speculations preoccupied many of the pious, who hoped to predict the coming conflict between good and evil and the advent of God's reign. Matthew's Gospel arranges the discourse in which Jesus discussed the coming judgment in such a way as to divert Matthew's contemporaries from paying too much attention to the destruction of the Temple in A.D. 70. In the verse immediately before this Sunday's gospel Jesus insisted that no one, not even Jesus in the mortal weakness he embraced to save us, could know the day and hour when heaven and earth would pass away (Mt 24:36). On the contrary, the cataclysm–the root meaning is "flood"–will surprise us. "In those days before the flood, they were eating and drinking, marrying and giving in marriage, up to the day that Noah entered the ark" (Mt 24:38). We think it is only a prolonged period of showers, but the end of history is seeping in at the corners, rising toward the doorsill. None of us lives very far from the end of the world. Paleolithic men and women met it at the edge of a sharpened stone ax. We meet it today after some time attached to elaborate life-support machinery, unless we are lucky and go quickly: "...one will be taken, and one will be left" (Mt 24:40, 41). The end of history for you and me is where we meet it. "Therefore, stay awake!" (Mt 24:42).

Saint Paul, writing to the Jewish Christian community of Rome that he had not yet met, urged watchfulness on them as well. "The night is advanced; the day is at hand" (Rom 13:12). Religious aliens uncomfortable in the violent culture of the capricious Emperor Nero, the Jewish Christians of Rome treasured Paul's letter and its exhortations for them to live "not in orgies and drunkenness, not in promiscuity and lust, not in rivalry and jealousy" (Rom 13:13). Wide-awake people will not allow thieves to break into their houses. The drunken and the debauched are easily rolled. St. Paul followed Jesus in urging us to sober up, to wake up. "...at an hour you do not expect, the Son of Man will come" (Mt 24:44).

So we die—what of it? People have always known that. What does revelation in the Jewish and Christian traditions have to add to what actuarial tables can statistically predict? A great deal: hope for the future. The first reading derives from the work of the eighth-century-B.C. prophet Isaiah. Living under lackluster kings of Judah, Isaiah looked forward to a time when Jerusalem and its Temple on Mount Zion would offer the world a beacon of truth about God and the divinely created order for humankind: "'Come, let us climb the Lord's mountain,/ to the house of the God of Jacob,/ that he may instruct us in his ways,/ and we may walk in his paths'" (Is 2:3).

The Temple of the eighth century B.C. did not offer much instruction to non-Judeans; the Yahweh-worshiping people of the northern kingdom, faced with imminent defeat by the Assyrians, sought the face of the Lord in their own local sanctuaries. Jerusalem, intended by David to be a capital and holy city open to northerners and southerners alike, had become distinctly southern over the two centuries since its Davidic conquest. Both Israelites (northerners) and Judeans (southerners) bore responsibility for this tragic division of the chosen people. At an even more basic level, Jews and Gentiles bear responsibility for the Babel of divisiveness that keeps humankind from the oneness that mirrors the Creator.

But Isaiah holds out hope for the future. In that future Yahweh "shall judge between the nations,/ and impose terms on many peoples./ They shall beat their swords into plowshares/ and their spears into pruning hooks" (Is 2:4). Advent begins with this vision of the future, this bold assertion that the coming of the Son of Man into our lives, individual and collective, can bring peace.

First Sunday of Advent (B)

Readings: Isaiah 63:16–17, 19; 64:2–7;
1 Corinthians 1:3–9; Mark 13:33–37

Future Challenges

Talk about the end of the world suggests to the American imagination the cartoon figure of a bearded fanatic wearing a sandwich board proclaiming the imminence of the "End." Jews, Christians and Muslims have, at various points in history, looked forward with a mixture of dread and hope to the consummation of time. As inheritors of a linear-historical rather than a cyclical-natural worldview, the descendants of Abraham travel in faith toward a future in which the just will receive their reward and the unjust their recompense. While Hindus and Buddhists conceive of existence as a wheel of timelessness from which, at best, escape or extinction can be achieved, those who trace their traditions of faith back to the arid hills and valleys of the Middle East are less convinced that nature will go on forever. Religion as an opiate derives naturally from the flood plains of Asia; religion as revolutionary fervor clings tenaciously to the barren rocks of Sinai, Judea and the Arabian peninsula. Dread of the future and hope for its unveiling–apocalypse–arise both from discomfort with the status quo and from injustices suffered by decent people at the hands of those who literally do not give a damn.

The temptation of the oppressed lies in the direction of trying to predict the day of their deliverance with calendrical precision. The contemporaries of Jesus, world-weary after a century of Roman occupation, looked for divine signals of their liberation by a savior anointed by God. Such an anointed one (messiah) had at times ruled Israel in the persons of Saul, David and Solomon. But the integrity of the monarchy degenerated rapidly, even within the reigns of those first three kings (1030–930 B.C.). The eighth-century-B.C. Isaiah held out some hope for such political messiahs as Hezekiah of Judah (716–687 B.C.), but all semblance of divinely anointed monarchy collapsed in Jerusalem a century later (587 B.C.).

Third Isaiah, the source of chapters 56 to 66 of the Book of Isaiah, reflects some time in the period of Persian hegemony over Jerusalem, perhaps the fifth century B.C., when the enthusiasm of Second Isaiah for the Persian liberation (Is 45) had cooled. The first reading for this Sunday mirrors this post-exilic Jewish disillusionment with the reality of their home-coming to the desolate city. The saved remnant no longer looks for human leadership arising on earth from the house of David but for divine intervention in history from on high: "Oh, that you would rend the heavens and come down" (Is 63:19b). Survivors of holocausts (Jewish, Armenian, Cambodian, Gypsy, Ukrainian, Bosnian, Southern Sudanese, Rwandan, to name but a few) can feel in their bones these lonely but impassioned words. Israel, the people singled out for God's special love, must sometimes have wondered whether he could not have spread his love around more evenly. But faith still triumphs over despair: "Yet, O LORD, you are...the potter:/ we are all the work of your hands" (Is 64:7). Notice, however, that the clay laments its brokenness.

Before Saul or David or Solomon had ruled God's people, Yahweh shepherded the flock alone, revealing the divine will through charismatic figures like Samuel and the other Judges. Psalm 80 (the responsorial psalm this Sunday) reflects

Israelite faith in the more-than-human rulership of God, even if that transcendent God must deal with us through a human being, "the son of man whom you yourself made strong" (Ps 80:18). Many candidates presented themselves to the Jewish masses of the first century A.D. as the hoped-for Son of man. The procuratorship of Pontius Pilate exacerbated messianic fervor; the breaking point was reached three decades later when the Zealot revolt led to the Roman devastation of the just-completed Temple. The gospel reading comes from the end of a discourse of Jesus in Mark in which he warns the disciples—and the later readers of Mark—not to be caught up in the apocalyptic enthusiasm of the Zealots.

Jesus demythologized those predictions of the day of messianic deliverance so common among his contemporaries: "Be watchful....You do not know when the time will come" (Mk 13:33). Jesus wanted his first disciples, and us, to rid ourselves of the temptation to predict the exact time of the end, to force God's plan of salvation into the timetables of human scheming. The Lord, like the master of the household, will come for all of us, or for any one of us, when we least expect, "whether in the evening, or at midnight, or at cockcrow, or in the morning" (Mk 13:35). As his servants, the keepers of his household, we are warned not to let him "come suddenly and find you sleeping" (Mk 13:36). Whether God comes back into our lives through nuclear disaster or a heart attack, God is surely coming.

In Saint Paul's terminology, as excerpted this Sunday from the opening of the First Epistle to the Corinthians, "the revelation of our Lord Jesus Christ" (1 Cor 1:7)—the apocalypse—has not yet happened, even in the death and resurrection of Jesus, although those events have begun to usher in the "day of our Lord" (1 Cor 1:8). Paul came to realize as his ministry continued that the advent of that day would be less predictable than the Zealots and other contemporary enthusiasts, Jewish and Christian, might have imagined.

Was the hope of Israel, the hope of the early church for the coming of the Messiah in glory a delusion? Did the Zoroastrians look in vain for Saoshyant, the deliverer from the battle of good and evil? Was the desire of Mahayana Buddhists for the coming of a future Buddha merely vain? "As we wait in joyful hope for the coming of our Savior Jesus Christ," as we say in the mass, are we kidding ourselves? Are we not all terminal patients, heading inexorably for death and extinction? Some pessimists think so. Karl Marx, most famously and eloquently, called all religion "the opium of the people," a painkiller that helps us ignore real pain. But those words of Marx, excerpted from the introduction to his *Contribution to the Critique of Hegel's Philosophy of Right*, deserve to be read in their fuller context. There is something about Marx's words on religion that makes me suspect he missed the messianic Judaism from which he derived at least some aspects of his thought:

> Religious distress is at the same time the expression of real distress. Religion is the sigh of the oppressed creature, the heart of a heartless world, just as it is the spirit of a spiritless situation. It is the opium of the people.

Is that entirely antireligious? It certainly is when it goes on to state that "the abolition of religion as the illusory happiness of the people is required for their real happiness....The criticism of religion is therefore in embryo the criticism of the vale of tears, the halo of which is religion." But Marx does seem to concede that there really is something behind religion, a real distress that cries out to heaven for redress.

Advent begins, not as so many shopping days till Christmas,

but as a radical reorientation of our eyes toward God's future, the full unveiling of the lordship and messiahship of Jesus. If the eschatologically prurient fall into error by trying to time God's future, most of us fall into the opposite vice, thinking God has only a past. Both as a church and as individuals we fall into a rut in our thinking about God, our thinking with God. We try to force God into categories of the past, ours and God's. In Advent we are called to look forward to God's future and our future with God.

First Sunday of Advent (C)

Readings: Jeremiah 33:14–16;
1 Thessalonians 3:12–4:2; Luke 21:25–28, 34–36

Raise Your Heads!

Only if you have lived through a civil war could you appreciate what happened in Jerusalem and the surrounding countryside in the late 60s and early 70s of the first century of the Christian era. The inhabitants of the Jewish capital during those years had divided themselves dramatically. The Zealot movement, supposedly united in its opposition to Roman colonialism, split into contending factions, the most inclined to terrorism called the *sicarii* by the Romans: "dagger-wielders." The Zealots themselves, at least in their origins, had begun as a nationalistic branch of the Pharisee movement, espousing purified Jewish observance. Some of the Sadducees appeared to be as patriotic as the Zealots, although the priest Joseph ben Matthias (Josephus) turned out to be a traitor to the Jewish cause while he was supposedly leading their forces in Galilee. The Jewish Christians–still perceived as a sect of Judaism with some Gentile adherents–abandoned Jerusalem in its moment of crisis and began the long and sad process of alienation from the parent stock. The Romans ultimately took the city after nearly starving out its citizens. The recently completed Temple of Herod was destroyed and Jerusalem began to lose its identity as the Holy City. After another and even more bloody Jewish revolt in the 130s, Jerusalem was renamed Aelia Capitolina and Jews were officially denied entrance to the city until the Muslim Arabs conquered it in the seventh century A.D.

Jesus and his contemporaries, living with the beginnings of the divisions that sundered Jewish society a few decades later, realized that confrontation with the overwhelming power of Rome could only spell doom for the homeland of Yahwistic faith. Remembering the horrors of the Syrian-Greek (Seleucid) persecution in the second century B.C. and fearing that no equivalent of the united Maccabean force could halt it, Jesus took the Jeremiah option in politics. To the disappointment not only of his more patriotic disciples but also of some modern enthusiasts who would like to redecorate him in revolutionary garb, Jesus shied away from interpreting the Roman-Jewish confrontation as the end of the world. The gospel selection from Luke for this first Sunday in a new liturgical year follows a section in which Jesus is portrayed as interpreting the destruction of Jerusalem in terms somewhat short of eschatological.

Not that Jesus or Luke denied the possibility of an end to the world as they knew it. "On earth nations will be in dismay, perplexed by the roaring of the sea and the waves. People will die of fright in anticipation of what is coming upon the world, for the powers of the heavens will be shaken" (Lk 21:25–26). More than one human generation over the past two millennia has felt that its time and place fitted that description of the end of times. The fact is that every human generation has recognized and will continue to recognize around it the symptoms of self-destruction, the collective suicide of a world bent on worshiping itself as an iron-eyed god. Into each generation arrives "the Son of Man coming in a cloud with power and great glory" (Lk 21:27). We all stand under the judgment of the Son of Man, the perfect human being in whom the fullness of Godhood stands revealed. At your death and mine we will taste the sacrament of the endtime, as much of the endtime as any mortal can comprehend.

Given the delay of the end of times for two millennia , what should the faithful disciple of Jesus do with the chaos in which we live? "Stand erect and raise your heads because your redemption is at hand" (Lk 21:28). Our more craven instincts bid us to crouch down and duck our heads, antici- pating the worst. But Jesus faced up to his endtime with courage, and so must we: "That day will assault everyone who lives on the face of the earth. Be vigilant..." (Lk 21:35). The disciples in Gethsemane found it difficult to keep watch with Jesus as he confronted the end, and so do we. But God can still graciously make it possible for us "to stand before the Son of Man" (Lk 21:36). That is what we mean by faith in the face of death.

The media seldom headline an outbreak of peace, mainly

because human beings find ways to prevent peace from happening. The collapse of worldwide communism has not yet promoted coexistence between every wolf and lamb on earth. The internal turmoil of so many former Soviet and Third World countries remind us that "nations will be in dismay" for a while to come. History has not ended quite yet.

Does that mean that the Son of man is coming soon? Millenarian sects always try to read contemporary events in a gnostic fashion, promoting the idea that all our problems have a simple solution: The end is coming! The certitudes of millenarians fade when the predicted end does not come. Jesus and the majority of the New Testament writers tried to cool the enthusiasm of their contemporaries for such easy solutions to complicated problems. "That day [will] catch you by surprise like a trap" (Lk 21:34). The point of a trap is that the one to be entrapped cannot predict when it will snap shut. Other gospel passages compare the coming of the end and the advent of the glorious Messiah to the unexpected arrival of one's boss or the nighttime activity of a burglar. If it could be predicted, it wouldn't really be the end.

"Beware," Jesus and Luke told their contemporaries, "that your hearts do not become drowsy from carousing and drunkeness and the anxieties of daily life" (Lk 21:34). Every age has its own forms of such obliviousness. For many Americans today, the Messiah's advent may interrupt the schedule on prime-time television. One may speculate how CNN will cover the end of the world as we know it. On the other hand, CNN may already be doing so. The world ends every day, not only for those who die that day, but also for those of us who survive, one day closer to the end. Whether we reach the end tonight or many millennia from tonight, we will reach an end: "Pray that you have the strength to escape the tribulations that are imminent and to stand before the

Son of Man" (Lk 21:36). Not bad advice for beings inextricably caught up in the process of time, secular and sacred.

The first reading derives from a late contribution to the work of the prophet Jeremiah in which God promises to "raise up for David a just shoot" (Jer 33:15). Reflecting on the collapsed house of David, the author obviously recognized that justice dwindled as the generations passed. With the future descendant of David, "Judah shall be safe/ and Jerusalem shall dwell secure" (Jer 33:16). In an age obsessed with national and international security, we can recognize our ancestry in this prophetic passage. But no political leader in Israel or anywhere else can provide the security for which we long. Both Isaiah and Jeremiah recognized that in Yahweh alone lay the true safety of the chosen people.

Paul, writing the earliest of his letters to Christian communities, still expected the royal advent (parousia) of the risen and ascended Jesus in the near future. He outlived that naive expectation, but not the sense of urgency that it introduced into his apostolic life. The coming of the Son of Man was pictured as a royal visitation. Paul prays for the Thessalonians at the beginning of the sixth decade of the first century A.D.: "May the Lord...strengthen your hearts, to be blameless in holiness before our God and Father at the coming of our Lord Jesus with all his holy ones" (1 Thes 3:12–13). We can take comfort in the fact that Jesus will not come alone, but will have with him a company of the saints. Surely somewhere in that crowd we will know someone who can put in a good word for us. The Christian reaction to the coming judgment should not be fear but courageous love: "May the Lord make you increase and abound in love for one another and for all, just as we have for you" (1 Thes 3:12). Lovelessness ducks its head when troubles come over the world and close in on us

"...*a shoot shall sprout....*" (Is 11:1)

"like a trap" (Lk 21:34). Love takes risks, stands up straight and raises its head. Advent begins on this happy note.

Monday of the First Week of Advent

Readings: Isaiah 2:1–5 (or Isaiah 4:2–6);
Matthew 8:5–11

Across First Avenue from the New York headquarters of the United Nations you can read on a wall the biblical aspirations of at least some of the founders of that international organization. Those words, more or less the same in the prophecy of Micah (4:1–3) and at the beginning of Isaiah, occur in this first Monday of Advent's first reading (except when they have already been read the day before in Cycle A, in which case Isaiah 4: 2–6 is substituted). "They shall beat their swords into plowshares/ and their spears into pruning hooks;/ One nation shall not raise the sword against another,/ nor shall they train for war again" (Is 2:4). In view of recent military activities undertaken in the name of the United Nations, it might have proven helpful to inscribe those words on a turnable signboard, each side with opposite sentiments, an excerpt from the prophet

Joel complementing Isaiah's and Micah's words of peace: "Beat your plowshares into swords,/ and your pruning hooks into spears;/ let the weak man say, 'I am a warrior!'" (Jl 4:10).

Whatever the faults of the United Nations in actual practice, the idea behind its foundation in 1945 has stood the test of time. Neo-isolationists are still denouncing the U.N. as they were in the 1950s, but the world community has largely come to recognize its value. The author of this passage in the early books of Isaiah had seen through the mythology of isolationism, the Judah-firstism evident in other parts of the thirty-nine chapters of First Isaiah. In this passage, at least, the prophet's vision of Jerusalem's future hails the holy city as a place of pilgrimage not only for Jews but for Gentiles as well: "All nations shall stream toward it" (Is 2:2). But all of this universalism lay in the future for Isaiah; it had not yet come to pass. But he looked forward to a time of universal peace governed by Yahweh from his Temple throne: "He shall judge between the nations,/ and impose terms on many peoples" (Is 2:4).

The alternate reading from Isaiah also reflects a theology of hope. "The branch of the LORD" and "the fruit of the earth" signal hope "for the survivors of Israel" (Is 4:2). The prophet sees the travails of Jerusalem as an experience of purgation preceding a new exodus when Yahweh's glory will once more cover his people with "a smoking cloud by day/ and a light of flaming fire by night" (Is 4:5). But this time the divine glory will settle not on a wandering population but on "the whole site of Mount Zion/ and over her place of assembly" (Is 4:5).

The hopes of Isaiah for Jerusalem as a religious focus not only for Jews but for Gentiles as well met their New Testament equivalent in the hopes expressed by Jesus for a Roman centurion who begged him to heal his paralyzed servant. The Gentile centurion, charged with a small Roman military garrison in Capernaum, realized that a devout Jew like

Jesus might be reluctant to enter into a household that might bring on him ritual pollution, although Jesus had readily agreed to do so. The centurion's words have for many centuries preceded the reception of communion in Latin Catholic practice: "I am not worthy to have you enter under my roof" (Mt 8:8). A military man to the core, the centurion presumed that Jesus has authority to give orders to unruly spirits like his servant's sickness and could effect the healing without entering a Gentile household. Jesus was astounded by the self-abasement of this non-Jewish military man: "Amen, I say to you," Jesus declared, "in no one in Israel have I found such faith" (Mt 8:10). Tragic as these words were for the Jewish contemporaries of Jesus, Gentiles can only rejoice in the extraordinary humility of that nameless Roman centurion and the extraordinary generosity of the Lord of Israel made flesh.

Tuesday of the First Week of Advent

Readings: Isaiah 11:1–10; Luke 10:21–24

One could probably date the origins of American Catholics who went to parochial school by whether they could enumerate the seven gifts of the Holy Spirit or not. The more advanced also knew the twelve fruits of the Holy Spirit. For better or worse, Catholics who grew up after the Second Vatican Council memorized less, although they not infrequently had thought more about the Holy Spirit and, thanks to the charismatic renewal, had even experienced the Spirit's gifts in multiple forms. The traditional theological and catechetical list of the seven gifts of the Holy Spirit derives from the Book of Isaiah in the Septuagint (the Greek version of the Hebrew Bible). The Hebrew text of today's first reading mentions only six gifts, in three pairs: (1) wisdom and understanding, (2) counsel and strength, (3) knowledge and fear of the Lord. The orphaned seventh, piety, came to birth after the prophetic career of Isaiah.

The gifts of the Spirit in Isaiah manifest themselves particularly in the heir of the house of Jesse, the father of King David, for whom Isaiah—frustrated with the de facto rulers of Judah—looked with ardent longing. The first reading sketches an ideal portrait of a future, peaceable kingdom ruled by this descendant of Jesse. The author of this prophecy had lived to see the royal house of David, the tree that sprang from the root of Jesse, reduced to a stump. But the prophet still had hope that God could do something even with such an unpromising remnant of a glorious past: "A shoot shall sprout from the stump of Jesse,/ and from his roots a bud shall blossom" (Is 11:1). The breath of God will descend on that stump and make the new shoot into a perfect king: "Not by appearance shall he judge,/ nor by hearsay shall he decide,/ But he shall judge the poor with justice/ and decide aright for the land's afflicted" (Is 11:3–4). The ideal king of Isaiah's desires, probably the son of Ahaz, Hezekiah (r. 716–687 B.C.), turned out to be less ideal than the prophet had hoped.

The poor and the afflicted are still waiting for that final and perfect Advent, as are we all. The gospel passage from Luke gives a glimpse of Jesus rejoicing in the Holy Spirit, the gift of the Father. In Jesus we have access to the Father: "No one knows who the Son is except the Father, and who the Father is except the Son and anyone to whom the Son wishes to reveal him" (Lk. 10:22). The Holy Spirit in which our ideal King Jesus rejoiced enabled him to praise his Father and enables us as well to enter into that joyful dialogue of Father and Son. Hezekiah may have disappointed Isaiah in the long run, but Jesus will never disappoint.

Wednesday of the First Week of Advent

Readings: Isaiah 25:6–10; Matthew 15:29–37

If you normally ate indoors as a child (like most Americans), eating outdoors was a treat–a picnic. Although in its original sense the picnic was more like what Americans today call a potluck supper, eventually its quality as an outdoor meal predominated in its definition, ants and all. As early as the Book of Exodus Yahweh summoned Moses and a few companions to seal the Sinai covenant with him on a mountaintop throne room of God where they ate and drank (Ex 24:9–11) at a picnic both divine and human.

This image of the beginning of Yahweh's communal feast with Israel shaped as well their hope for its consummation, the feast on the mountain to which the first reading from Isaiah points: "On this mountain the LORD of hosts/ will provide for all peoples/ a feast of rich food and choice wines,/ juicy, rich food and pure, choice wines" (Is 25:6). The responsorial psalm (23) locates Yahweh's picnic "in verdant pastures," in view of the fact that those eating outdoors are pictured as sheep of a divine Shepherd, although human picnickers seem to be expected when "you spread the table before me/ in the sight of my foes" (Ps 23:5).

Mark and Matthew each give us two accounts of Jesus feeding multitudes; Luke and John each narrate this story once. The eschatological banquet to which Jesus made reference at the Last Supper (Mt 26:29; Mk 14:25; Lk 22:18), a recollection of both the picnic in Exodus and that in Isaiah, featured a great deal of wine. Only John (2:1–11) remembers Jesus in a context of celebration with abundant wine. The accounts of the multiplication of loaves and fishes in every instance emphasize the bread and forget about the fishes. Why? Perhaps because "the breaking of bread" (Acts 2:42) became so central to the communal celebrations of the early church. Each gospel narrative of the multiplication of the loaves falls into phrases more familiar from the accounts of the Last Supper: "He...gave thanks, broke the loaves, and gave them to the disciples, who in turn gave them to the crowds" (Mt 15:36). The coming of the Messiah and the messianic banquet he inaugurated may well provide the reason why families come together for the abundance of Christmas dinner year after year.

Thursday of the First Week of Advent

Readings: Isaiah 26:1–6; Matthew 7:21, 24–27

"Next year in Jerusalem!" Jews pledge at the end of the Passover seder, a pledge they continued to enunciate during many centuries of enforced diaspora. Even though Israel as a nation had existed long before Jerusalem was taken from the Jebusites by King David (2 Sm 5:6–10), it was meant to serve as a neutral capital for both the northern Israelites and the southern people of Judah. The degeneration of the line of David–with Solomon becoming despotic–ensured the northerners' secession, and Jerusalem remained the capital of all Israel in theory only. Although the northerners also worshiped Yahweh at their ancient shrines, they found it easy at these shrines to mix with their Yahwism not a little of the worship of Baal and other deities.

Isaiah, God's spokesman on Jerusalem as *the* sacred center for all Israel, reflects this political theology in the first reading: "A strong city have we;/ he sets up walls and ramparts to protect us..../Trust in the Lord forever!/ For the Lord is an eternal rock" (Is 26:1, 4). The rocky hillock on which the Temple was built, Mount Zion, has always played a central role in the Jewish imagination, ancient and modern. Mount Zion was the goal of every Jewish pilgrim and the goal, as well, of modern political Zionism. Psalm 118, the source of the responsorial verses, appears in the psalter at the end of a series of psalms

(113–18) used liturgically by Jews who came up to Jerusalem for the great feasts of Passover, Weeks and Tabernacles. Even in the scant excerpts in the responsorial psalm one can hear the prayerful words of the pilgrims ("Open to me the gates of justice;/ I will enter them and give thanks to the LORD.") and the welcoming words of the Temple priests ("Blessed is he who comes in the name of the LORD" [Ps 118:19, 26]).

Isaiah and the Jerusalem psalmist find that Jesus has a different foundation in mind for the kingdom of God that is coming. Yahweh's Temple on Mount Zion did not, in the long run, keep Jerusalem from devastation. The city was destroyed more than once. But the new holy city, the kingdom of God that Jesus proclaimed, would be founded on something more solid: "Everyone who listens to these words of mine and acts on them will be like a wise man who built his house on rock" (Mt 7:24). The words of Jesus (enfleshing the word of God) accepted in faith and carried out in love make a religious foundation very different from a sacred city or sacred place.

Friday of the First Week of Advent

Readings: Isaiah 29:17–24; Matthew 9:27–31

If you have lived through a coup d'etat in a Third World country, you will know the exhilaration that sometimes greets the change from a dictatorship to something new. Alas, when that "something new" degenerates into yet another dictatorship, as is too often the case, the despair that settles on the hapless citizens of such countries knows no bounds. The excerpt from Isaiah in the first reading today reflects something like the exhilaration people experience after a welcome coup d'etat. Just before this passage the prophet had pronounced woes upon Jerusalem, about to be surrounded by its enemies, the instruments of God's wrath (Is 29:1–10). After further excoriation of Jerusalem for its infidelity (Is 29:11–16) the prophet suddenly breaks into the proclamation of consolation for Jerusalem, reflecting, perhaps, the reversal of Jerusalem's fortunes that occurred when the Assyrian army that had besieged Jerusalem was laid low by heaven-sent disease (2 Kgs 19:35).

Among the wonders associated with that reversal of fortunes Isaiah counts the healing of the deaf and the blind: "On that day the deaf shall hear/ the words of a book;...the eyes of the blind shall see" (Is 29:18). Matthew's Gospel presents us with a similar image, the reversal of fortunes effected by the advent of Jesus into the lives of two blind men in Capernaum.

The two blind men petitioned Jesus with an obviously messianic title: "Son of David, have pity on us!" (Mt 9:27). Jesus tended to shy away from this highly political description of his status, and he seems to have ignored the two blind men at first until they followed him to the house where he was staying. He questioned their faith that he could cure them, but they assured him that they did have such faith, something that went beyond the hopes of political messianism. Touching their sightless eyes, he declared, "Let it be done for you according to your faith" (Mt 9:29), but he warned them (fruitlessly, the evangelist remarks) to tell no one how their sight was restored.

All restorations of sight, hearing and speech in the New Testament serve to point to the greater healing Jesus really came to accomplish: the restoration of faith in or fidelity to God in the hearts of God's people. It was this prior faith of the two blind men, a faith that included insight into Jesus as more than a political messiah, that restored their sight.

Saturday of the First Week of Advent

Readings: Isaiah 30:19–21, 23–26;
Matthew 9:35–10:1, 6–8

The aridity of most of the Middle East has affected the imagination of the people who live in that area: Their vision of past or future beatitude conjures up a well-watered, enclosed garden (a paradise), and their vision of past or future banishment centers either on a burning garbage heap (Gehenna) or a barren desert. The first reading for this final day of the first week of Advent envisions Yahweh's graciousness to Jerusalem, then and now a place challenged with water and food supply problems, as providing them with abundance of both: "The Lord will give you the bread you need and the water for which you thirst..../He will give rain for the seed/ that you sow in the ground,/ and the wheat that the soil produces/ will be rich and abundant" (Is 30: 20, 23).

Jesus, like Yahweh in Isaiah's prophecy, took pity not so much on Jerusalem and its elite population as on the "the crowds...troubled and abandoned, like sheep without a shepherd" (Mt 9:36). Knowing that his work of healing and exorcism had to continue beyond the mortal lifetime implicit in his coming to us in flesh and blood, Jesus had pity on crowds down the centuries and across many borders, appointing his disciples to continue his work. But he instructed them at first to concentrate on proclaiming the news of God's reign to "the lost sheep of the house of Israel" (Mt 10:6). These words immediately follow a series of miracles and precede a discourse aimed at the disciples, who will continue the work of Jesus. Like Jesus they are to do this work not as a business but as a manifestation of God's pity: "Without cost you have received; without cost you are to give" (Mt 10:8).

The
Second
Week
of
Advent

"...a highway for our God!" (Is 40:3)

Second Sunday of Advent (A)

Readings: Isaiah 11:1–10; Romans 15:4–9;
Matthew 3:1–12

Hope

Pope John XXIII celebrated the Rome Olympic Games of
1960 by having a commemorative medallion struck. Pointing
to the fact that the youthful athletes of 1960 had been born,
for the most part, during World War II, the medallion featured
the image of a stump from which a fresh new twig was
sprouting. For all the horrors of the Nazi concentration camps,
Stalingrad, Hiroshima and Nagasaki, Iwo Jima and the Battle of
the Bulge, some parents and children had survived. Abebe
Bikila, the Ethiopian long-distance runner, outpaced all his
competitors barefoot through the streets of the Eternal City.
Cassius Marcellus Clay, as the eighteen-year-old American then
was known, began his career as a boxer of world renown. John

XXIII, the survivor of many wars—military, diplomatic and ecclesiastical—blessed the Olympic athletes with hope in his heart for the future. He died a hero three years later, after the first skirmishes of the uphill battle he began himself, the Second Vatican Council.

The papal Olympic medallion derived its imagery from the first reading for this Sunday. Isaiah the prophet, frustrated with the mediocrity of the Davidic royal line in eighth-century Jerusalem, still held out hope for the future of those descendants of Jesse. Jesse himself had been surprised that his youngest and least significant son proved to be the choice of God and Samuel as anointed ruler of Israel (1 Sm 16:4–13). Isaiah hoped that the youthful son of Ahaz, Hezekiah (r. 715–687 B.C.), would do a better job than his father. He did, but his son Manasseh (r. 687–642 B.C.) undid his father's accomplishments. Isaiah's prophetic hope for a future king foundered on the de facto descendants of Jesse. With the total collapse of monarchy in Jerusalem a century after Hezekiah's death, devout Jews came to look to a more distant future for the advent of a ruler in whose reign "the wolf shall be the guest of the lamb,/ and the leopard shall lie down with the kid" (Is 11:6).

Saint Paul, writing to a mixed congregation of Jewish and Gentile Christians in Rome, tried to mediate in the disputes that divided them regarding the relevance of the Jewish Law and especially the dietary regulations. Some of those Christians, deeply convinced of their freedom from the need to observe such prescriptions once they had been redeemed by the Messiah Jesus, flaunted that freedom in the face of others who felt religiously uncomfortable with such an unregulated life. Paul urged both factions, the liberals and conservatives of their day and church, to exercise restraint. Both the observant and the nonobservant were to revere the

Jewish scriptures, something that Marcion and the earliest Christian heretics found it difficult to accept. These scriptures, Paul insisted, were "written for our instruction, that by endurance and by the encouragement of the Scriptures we might have hope" (Rom 15:4). The reign of Manasseh did not invalidate Isaiah's hope for a future Son of David; the relativization of the Law did not cancel out the importance of the biblical tradition.

But those Roman Christians who observed *kashrut* (the rules of kosher diet) and those who did not–and not all the former were converted Jews nor were all the latter converted Gentiles–had to learn to "welcome one another, then, as Christ welcomed you, for the glory of God" (Rom 15:7). A good Advent lesson for all stripes of contemporary Catholics and contemporary Christians! In the kingdom that is yet to come there will be no right or left wings, only a passionately held middle: "The calf and the young lion shall browse together,/ with a little child to guide them" (Is 11:6).

The Dead Sea Scrolls, discovered in 1947 in the Wadi Qumran on the West Bank of the Jordan, tell us about the dissident Jewish religious community from which these scrolls emanated. Jewish pietists unhappy with the Jerusalem priesthood in the post-Maccabean era, the sectarians of Qumran withdrew to the wilderness of Judea east of Jerusalem and strove for an ideal of perfect priestly ritual purity. Their written remains indicate that a verse from the beginning of the Second Isaiah inspired their desert existence: "In the desert prepare the way of the LORD" (Is 40:3).

The sectarians of the Wadi Qumran may not have been the only dissident Jews to betake themselves to that otherwise unattractive habitat. Dissidents from the Wadi Qumran community may even have included no less a figure than John the Baptist ("Baptizer" in the 1970 edition of the New American

Bible, aimed perhaps at those who may have thought he was not a Roman Catholic!). The dominant preacher of the Advent season, John the Baptist differed from the Qumran sectarians in his apparent indifference to questions of ritual purity. The purity he sought and symbolized with his ritual baptism in the Jordan had much more to do with questions of social justice and the imminent rule of God. Unlike the sectarians of Qumran, John dealt with the Sadducees, the priestly class in Jerusalem, and the pious mainline lay group known as Pharisees. But he did not deal very diplomatically with his listeners: "You brood of vipers! Who warned you to flee from the coming wrath? Produce good fruit as evidence of your repentance" (Mt 3:7–8).

John the Baptist prefigured Jesus in many ways, not least of them in the basic thrust of his preaching: "Repent, for the kingdom of heaven is at hand" (Mt 3:2). But John cut a more eccentric figure than did Jesus. Modeling his style on the prophet Elijah, John dressed in "clothing made of camel's hair," not to be confused with a camel's hair coat. An early natural foods enthusiast, "his food was locusts and wild honey" (Mt 3:4). People later criticized Jesus for his more luxurious diet: "The Son of Man came eating and drinking and they said, 'Look, he is a glutton and a drunkard, a friend of tax collectors and sinners'" (Mt 11:19). John took a different path.

Harsh as the desert of Judea in which he preached, John confronted the religious leaders of his time, lay (Pharisees) and clerical (Sadducees). Professional religiousness would never save them from "the coming wrath" (Mt 3:7). John's baptism of repentance or reform prepared them for another baptism, much more effective. The one for whom John prepared his contemporaries "will baptize you with the holy Spirit and fire" (Mt 3:11). No amount of religious rhetoric on the part of preachers, no amount of spiritual experience among devotees can substitute for the entry of God into our lives. "His winnowing fan is in his hand. He will clear his threshing floor, and gather his wheat into his barn, but the chaff he will burn with unquenchable fire" (Mt 3:12) John the Baptist announced the advent of a King who proclaimed life where we had presumed death, who brought spring where we had expected winter.

Second Sunday of Advent (B)

Readings: Isaiah 40:1–5; 2 Peter 3:8–14; Mark 1:1–8

Interior Roadwork

In Third World countries a sure sign that the head of state or some other bigwig will soon visit a remote rural locality can be discerned in feverish activity by local authorities to repair the roads. In some American cities as well, the filling of potholes has political implications: the advent of municipal elections. Both types of road rehabilitation, prior to a ruler's visit or the day of judgment for officeholders, shed light on the readings in this Sunday's liturgy of the word. Our ruler is coming; on that day we will be judged on our conduct in office.

The Babylonian exile (587–538 B.C.) of the Judean remnant

of ancient Israel seemed at first like the doom of the people of God. What the Lord had forged through the hand of Moses in the Exodus from Egypt met its reversal when the captive Jews from the Promised Land left for the Mesopotamian capital. But forty-eight years after the desolation of Jerusalem, Cyrus the Great, the new strongman of the Middle East, subdued Babylon and included it in the Persian empire. One year later Cyrus issued an edict allowing the Judeans to return to Jerusalem to live, with limited autonomy, in the land of their ancestors.

Second Isaiah saw in this imperial benevolence an act of God. The prologue to his prophetic work, from which the first reading derives, pictures the heavenly court in session and God (not at all unlike Cyrus) decreeing the release of Jerusalem from bondage. In the imagery of Second Isaiah, as in Ezekiel, both the Judeans and their God have languished in exile. Now, in the manner of a great emperor, Yahweh begins a royal progress back toward Jerusalem. The rough terrain between Babylon and Jerusalem must be prepared for the triumphant home journey of the God of Israel: "In the desert prepare the way of the LORD!/ Make straight in the wasteland a highway for our God!" (Is 40:3). Unlike Cyrus or even the now discredited Davidic monarchs, Yahweh conducted his royal progress without pomp and circumstance: "Like a shepherd he feeds his flock;/ in his arms he gathers the lambs" (Is 40:11). Second Isaiah is called to herald the good news: both Israel and Yahweh were returning to Jerusalem.

The Second Letter of Peter, very possibly the last written document in the New Testament, exhorts its second-century readers not to lose their perspective on the glorious coming of the Lord as King, the parousia. After the first Christian generations died, expectation of the imminent return of the risen and ascended Jesus cooled. The author, in this homily in the

Petrine tradition, assures his readers that "the Lord does not delay his promise" (2 Pt 3:9). Rather, what seems like cancellation is actually merciful postponement. Employing the usual Jewish-Christian imagery for apocalyptic divine judgment, the author urges us in every age "to be found without spot or blemish before him, at peace" (2 Pt 3:14). There is still time left to fill in the potholes!

Mark's account casts John the Baptist, the precursor, in the late prophetic role of God's messenger (Mal 3:1), or even of Elijah returned (Mal 4:1). Like Second Isaiah, John the Baptist was commissioned to prepare the Lord's way in the desert. Like the Qumran sectarians who withdrew from the Temple worship in Jerusalem in the late second century B.C. to the wilderness near the Dead Sea, John the Baptist understood the words of Second Isaiah to mean that the faithful should withdraw to the desert to prepare themselves for the coming of the Lord. John the Baptist summoned his contemporaries, not to the Dead Sea, but to the Jordan, where he urged on them a symbolic bath of repentance for their sins.

Modern historical studies of John the Baptist, about whom we have other sources (such as the Jewish historian Josephus) as well as the gospels, suggest that John the Baptist did more than prepare the way for Jesus. Even the gospels hint that John had his own agenda and found himself, imprisoned by Herod Antipas, a trifle nonplussed by what he heard in prison of the ministry of Jesus (Mt 11:2–29; Lk 7:18–35). After all, John had landed in prison for excoriating the notable family-values deficit in the household of Herod Antipas, who had taken his brother's wife as his bride. It is hard to imagine Jesus, who asked who would cast the first stone at the woman caught in adultery (Jn 8:7), dragging the marital problems of Herod Antipas and Herodias into public view. The Japanese Catholic novelist Shusaku Endo maintains in his *Life of Jesus* that John's image of God was of a harsh and forbidding father while Jesus, whose parentage was different, thought of God in more maternal terms. There still seem to be heirs of John the Baptist in certain nooks and crannies of the church.

Whatever the facts of the ministry of the historical John the Baptist, the gospels preserve what was most valuable, in Christian terms, of his work. Like Elijah, Second Isaiah and the messenger of God in Malachi, John (in Mark's account) was only a herald of "One mightier than I," who "will baptize you with the holy Spirit" (Mk 1:7–8). What does this expression signify? The God of Israel returned once more to Jerusalem in the advent of Jesus of Nazareth. But in this coming of the Lord, a new covenant was inaugurated, as Ezekiel had prophesied: "I will put my spirit within you and make you live by my statutes, careful to observe my decrees. You shall live in the land I gave your fathers; you shall be my people, and I will be your God" (Ez 36:27–28). In this new covenant, Jesus did what no prophet could accomplish: He plunged his people into the depths of God's own holiness, the Holy Spirit. Prophets only prepare the way for the Lord; Jesus is the Way of the Lord. Immersed (baptized) into Jesus, filled with the Holy Spirit, we enter into a new relationship with God, "new heavens and a new earth" (2 Pt 3:13).

Plunged into the life of God by Jesus, we already live in the presence of the Lord in glory. Whether the world lasts for a long time or only a little longer, we should take the delay of judgment as a dying Irish relative of mine took his suffering with cancer: as a chance to "whitewash the house" before a visitor comes. That the Visitor will come is certain, like a thief in the night, to use the common imagery of New Testament apocalyptic. Second Isaiah and John the Baptist have set us examples of Advent living, the vocation of heralds for the Lord. Starting with our personal potholes, we Advent people must constantly ready our world for the coming of the Lord. We do not give up on the world; we strive to keep the Lord's highway in constant repair.

Second Sunday of Advent (C)

Readings: Baruch 5:1–9; Philippians 1:4–6, 8–11;
Luke 3:1–6

In the Desert

If you find yourself occasionally fed up with politicians and the clergy, rest assured that you have a friend and fellow sufferer in John the Baptist. The son of Zechariah the priest seems to have rebelled against his father's religion and politics and may even have joined, at least for a time, the pious but eccentric opposition, the Qumran priestly puritans. This devout community withdrew to the desert near the Dead Sea a century and a half earlier, apparently in protest against the Maccabean usurpation of the high priesthood. Deserts in the Middle East have always provided a refuge for those dissatisfied with the mediocrity (or worse) of urban existence, as the memories of Antony and Pachomius in early Christian Egypt and the Muslim rigorists of modern Egypt attest. In the desert of Judea the

Qumran sectarians developed a ritual life of their own, independent of the Temple in Jerusalem. According to their *Manual of Discipline*, this priestly sect went into the wilderness in fulfillment of the same text from Second Isaiah with which John the Baptist is identified in every gospel: "A voice cries out:/ In the desert prepare the way of the LORD!" (Is 40:3).

These Qumran sectarians (apparently the same as the Essenes described by the Jewish historian Josephus) practiced ritual lustrations and a common meal that bear some resemblance not only to orthodox Jewish usages like the washing of neophytes and the Passover seder but also to the New Testament rituals of baptism and the eucharist. Unlike the Essenes, however, John seems to have looked to a larger public with which he could share the message God gave him. In this John paid more attention than did the Essenes to Second Isaiah's hope that "all flesh shall see the salvation of God" (Lk 3:6). In next Sunday's gospel in this cycle, John is shown preaching not only to religious Jews but also to Jewish quislings or possibly Gentiles, the soldiers of the hated Roman occupation. The influence of John the Baptist may well have spread beyond the borders of Judea through the work of his disciples. In the Acts of the Apostles we read that Paul encountered disciples of John the Baptist as far away as Ephesus (in modern Turkey), possibly disciples or companions of the Alexandrian Jew Apollos, who only knew the baptism of John (Acts 19:1–7).

John began his career in a setting of social and moral collapse that will strike most moderns as contemporary. "In the fifteenth year of the reign of Tiberius Caesar," when the aging and perverse emperor had virtually retired to Capri and handed over the empire to his anti-Semitic lieutenant Sejanus, "when Pontius Pilate was governor of Judea" (Lk 3:1) and free to treat the hated Jews as vermin, the Jewish populace had no one to look to for help. Herod Antipas and Philip, his half brother, sons of Herod the Great (d. 4 B.C.), ruled Galilee and areas of what is modern Syria. Their brother Archelaus, who once had ruled Judea and Samaria, had been deposed by the Romans years earlier. So much for what remained of Jewish independence, totally reduced to Roman vassalage.

The evangelist Luke adds a mysterious detail to his dating of the appearance of John the Baptist, noting that it occurred when "Lysanias was tetrarch of Abilene" (Lk 3:1). Who was this Lysanias and why bring up Abilene, an area of Syria not particularly connected with Jewish history? Some scholars have suggested that Luke himself came from this area; others think that Luke made a mistake, misdating an earlier Lysanias of Abilene put to death by Antony and Cleopatra in 36 B.C. Perhaps this Lysanias is a more obscure successor of the earlier Lysanias, ruler of Abilene when John the Baptist's message reached both Jew and Gentile there when Luke was young.

Luke's final benchmark for the advent of the word of God to John the Baptist is "the high priesthood of Annas and Caiaphas" (Lk 3:2). Father-in-law and son-in-law, these two figures epitomized for the gospel writers the craven subservience of the Jerusalem priesthood to Roman overlordship, the very sort of leadership that would drive the devout into the desert. All of these historical reference points lead up to the announcement that the word of God reached John the Baptist in the desert—the desert of Judea, surely, but also the desert of all Jewish hopes for historical success under God's protection. At a time of such apparent silence on the part of God, "the word of God came to John the son of Zechariah in the desert" (Lk 3:2). The noise of Jerusalem deafened its inhabitants to that still, small voice (1 Kgs 19:12), one better heard in the ultimate quiet of nature, a desert. That divine word urged John to undertake a mission of prophetic reform, "proclaiming a baptism of repentance for the forgiveness of sins" (Lk 3:3).

The first reading, from the Greek Old Testament book ascribed to Jeremiah's secretary Baruch, purports to be a prophecy of Jerusalem's restoration after the Babylonian exile. In fact, however, the sentiments expressed in this passage date from a later era, when Jews could be "gathered from the east and the west/ at the word of the Holy One" (Bar 5:5). In the last centuries before the time of John the Baptist and Jesus, some modern Jewish historians have suggested that Jews constituted nearly 10 percent of the population of the Greco-Roman world, most of them living outside the Holy Land. Whether they would return to Jerusalem from Rome or Babylon, from Alexandria or Damascus, these Jews would find that "God is leading Israel in joy/ by the light of his glory,/ with his mercy and justice for company" (Bar 5:9).

Paul, writing apparently from prison to the Christians of Philippi in Macedon, looked forward with them to what he called "the day of Christ Jesus" (Phil 1:6). For the primitive church, Jesus had only acceded to the title *Messiah* (Christ) in his resurrection from the dead, and that event would only fall into its historical context at the general resurrection. Meanwhile, Paul prayed that the Philippians and all his other newly founded communities of faith would be "filled with the fruit of righteousness that comes through Jesus Christ" (Phil 1:11).

Between the desert of John the Baptist and the harvest of justice hoped for by Paul, the graciousness of God and much human effort must intervene. How else can barren desert be reclaimed? It is not only in Lent that the church dresses in violet and reflects on the centrality of a baptism of repentance that leads to the forgiveness of sins.

Monday of the Second Week of Advent

Readings: Isaiah 35:1–10; Luke 5:17–26

The accommodation for the physically handicapped at entries, staircases and other types of public facilities in the United States over the last few decades has advanced at an uneven pace, state by state and municipality by municipality. Nevertheless, no matter how uneven the provision of such accommodations has been in the developed world, the almost complete lack of such accommodation in the developing world strikes the American who travels to such places. The small contributions one can give to handicapped beggars cannot do very much to alleviate the pain and humiliation they must live with day by day, and especially in societies that consider such disabilities merely unavoidable fate, or worse, punishment for sin.

Attempting to picture the joy that will break out when Yahweh's people return to Jerusalem, the prophet Isaiah (sounding very much like Second Isaiah) mentions among the wonders that will accompany their progress across the desert toward Zion that "Then will the eyes of the blind be opened,/ the ears of the deaf be cleared;/ Then will the lame leap like a stag,/ then the tongue of the dumb will sing" (Is 35:5–6). It is important to notice that these wonders will be signs that God "comes with vindication" (Is 35:4). Is it too far-fetched to think that Yahweh will not only vindicate exiled Judeans but also the despised disabled?

The gospel reading is Luke's version of the story also told by Mark and Matthew of how Jesus not only cured a paralytic but also forgave his sins. In John's Gospel Jesus denied that the man born blind was suffering for either his own sins or those of his parents (Jn 9:2–3), but many of his contemporaries thought differently. Paralysis still serves us as an image of what happens to a person crippled both physically and spiritually by addictive habits. Without falling into the prescientific fallacy of identifying paralysis with sin, even the paralyzed are capable of sin, and Jesus realized this in his encounter with this man let down through the roof into the midst of an indoor crowd. Whatever the sources of his sin and of his paralysis, Jesus also saw "their faith" (Lk 5:20)–the faith of the paralytic and that of his litter bearers, to say nothing of the faith of the unmentioned householder whose roof had just been cut open. Responding to that faith, Jesus extended to the paralytic both forgiveness of the unseen sin and healing for the very obvious paralysis. The authority with which he did both of these things, the first of which involved divine authority, astounded all the onlookers, some of them quite malevolent "scribes and Pharisees" (Lk 5:21), who saw in this unbinding of a paralytic not Yahweh's vindication of both the paralytic and his healer but blasphemy.

Tuesday of the Second Week of Advent

Readings: Isaiah 40:1–11; Matthew 18:12–14

Most urban Americans have little knowledge of sheep for obvious reasons, unless they have taken their children to petting zoos or traveled extensively in sheep-raising areas. The first thing that struck me about sheep in Africa, when I first lived there, was their lack of wool (they have adapted to the weather) and the ease with which, at any distance, they can be confused with goats. But I soon learned the difference between sheep and goats. The former are very stupid and the latter very smart: One seldom hits a goat with a car, but sheep prove more problematic on the road. Note that both Old Testament and New Testament compare God's people to sheep, not goats.

Second Isaiah opens his contribution to the Hebrew Bible with a call narrative: the singling out of the prophet, or even a company of prophets, to deliver good news to desolate Jerusalem and God's people at the conclusion of the Babylonian exile. The basic good news or gospel of Second Isaiah centers on the proclamation that Yahweh will resume his kingship over Israel, no longer ceding it to the discredited descendants of David: "Here comes with power/ the Lord God,/ who rules by his strong arm" (Is 40:10). Strong-arm rule may sound rather intimidating, but the prophet reminds us that Yahweh's strong arm is that of a gentle shepherd: "Like a shepherd he feeds his flock;/ in his arms he gathers the lambs,/ Carrying them in his bosom,/ and leading the ewes with care" (Is 40:11).

Matthew, Luke and John all preserve memorable portraits of Jesus as the good shepherd, perhaps because Jesus so characterized his Father in parable: like Father, like Son. The parable of what I can only call the incautious shepherd—who leaves ninety-nine sheep in the hills to search for one stray—demonstrates not only the overwhelming generosity of God but also the personal, individualizing nature of his love. "In just the same way, it is not the will of your heavenly Father that one of these little ones be lost" (Mt 18:14). In the context of this parable, Jesus was excoriating those who lead children astray, but the same could be said as well of those who lead astray the simple or the uninstructed. The Davidic shepherds had led Israel and Judah astray, finally provoking Yahweh to resume the Shepherd role himself (see Ez 34:7–11). Jesus took that role upon himself not in mere political terms but in personal, yet world wide terms, specified in his concern for all of God's "little ones."

Wednesday of the Second Week of Advent

Readings: Isaiah 40:25–32; Matthew 11:28–30

Release from prison, release from the hospital, release from the army, release from debt, release from school: At one time or another each one of us has experienced, in smaller or larger ways, what the Jews experienced in their release from Babylonian captivity. Second Isaiah addresses God's people as they return to their homeland and questions them about any religious compromises they may have succumbed to in those dreary days in Babylon. Did they occasionally bow with their slave drivers to the celestial powers, the stars, which even some astrologically inclined Americans still regard with superstitious awe? Yahweh puts those celestial powers in their created place: "Lift up your eyes on high/ and see who has created these things:/ He leads out their army and numbers them,/ calling them all by name" (Is 40:26). Creator and commander-in-chief, Yahweh stands outside his creation, as in the first chapter of Genesis, and orders reality into existence. To an exhausted Jewish nation faced with the daunting task of beginning over again, God offers himself as a source of strength: "They that hope in the Lord will renew their strength,/ they will soar as with eagles' wings;/ They will run and not grow weary,/ walk and not grow faint" (Is 40:31).

In Matthew's Gospel Jesus offered himself as the source of divine strength: "Come to me, all you who labor and are burdened, and I will give you rest" (Mt 11:28). Much of what burdened the Jewish contemporaries of Jesus consisted in the Pharisaic interpretation of the Law, exemplified in their assimilation of plucking grain on the Sabbath to harvesting in the passage that immediately follows this one (Mt 12:1–8). Also burdensome was the alliance of the Sadducees with Roman imperial authority, the combination that brought Jesus to the cross. It may not seem an easy burden, but the cross of Jesus (Mt 10:38) proves to be lighter than the burdens imposed by other human beings.

Thursday of the Second Week of Advent

Readings: Isaiah 41:13–20; Matthew 11:11–15

Second Isaiah would have liked John the Baptist as the very model of what that prophet hoped the ideal postexilic Israelite would be, a single-minded puritan: "I will make of you a threshing sledge,/ sharp, new, and double-edged,/ To thresh the mountains and crush them,/ to make the hills like chaff./ When you winnow them, the wind shall carry them off/ and the storm shall scatter them" (Is 41:15–16). John the Baptist envisioned the one who would come after him in similar terms: "His winnowing fan is in his hand. He will clear his threshing floor and gather his wheat into the barn, but the chaff he will burn with unquenchable fire" (Mt 3:12). Both the greatness and the limitations of prophets can be seen in the way they envision God's future, sometimes imposing on it their own strengths and forgetting that God's ways are not human ways, even those of prophets.

Jesus, very different from what John the Baptist had expected, nevertheless recognized the greatness of John, a greatness implicitly superior to that of any figure in the Old Testament: "Among those born of women there has been none greater than John the Baptist." But for all John's prophetic greatness, "the least in the kingdom of heaven is greater than he" (Mt 11:11). This disconcerting evaluation of John seems to give with one hand and take away with the other. But it places John on the cusp between the two covenants, greater than anyone who has preceded him and yet not entirely imbued with the greatness that could only come with the advent of God's reign.

Among the most puzzling verses from the New Testament is the one that follows: "From the days of John the Baptist until now, the kingdom of heaven suffers violence, and the violent are taking it by force" (Mt 11:12). Perhaps what Jesus referred to was the violence stirred up by rival claimants to messianic status, political and violent agents of what they construed to be God's reign in the first century. Among them may be the obscure figures mentioned by Gamaliel in the Acts of the Apostles, Theudas and Judas the Galilean (Acts 5:35–37), and, possibly in connection with the latter, "the Galileans whose blood Pilate had mingled with the blood of their sacrifices" (Lk 13:1), and maybe even Barabbas (Lk 23:19). John the Baptist might have had some sympathy for such revolutionary threshing sledges and winnowing fans, not unlike Elijah, who made and unmade kings; but Jesus evinced little sympathy for the proponents of such violence. He was the first of those born, and laid in a manger, in a new understanding of the reign of God.

Friday of the Second Week of Advent

Readings: Isaiah 48:17–19; Matthew 11:16–19

In the more desertified parts of the Middle East, and especially where sand dunes shift and make steady progress on a journey difficult to achieve, celestial navigation may prove as valuable for the landbound as it normally does for those who sail the pathless ocean. Knowing what road you must follow, the way you are to go, serves as a central image in both the Bible and the Qur'an to illustrate that human beings must follow the will of God. The first New Testament name for Christianity is "the new way" (Acts 9:2). Second Isaiah urges his hearers not to look to the stars but to Yahweh to chart their progress back to a new and redeemed Jerusalem: "I, the LORD, your God,/ teach you what is for your good,/ and lead you on the way you should go" (Is 48:17). For later Judaism *halachah*—another word for "way"—was a type of *midrash* or studied commentary on a text of the Torah that served as the basis for Hebrew legal principles. The responsorial psalm, the first in the psalter, praises the path followed by the just: "Happy the man who follows not/ the counsel of the wicked/ Nor walks in the way of sinners" (Ps 1:1).

The two ways contrasted in the gospel reading are not those of the unjust and the just but those of John the Baptist and Jesus. Jesus recognized the cousinship between his own preaching of God's reign and that proclaimed by John the Baptist, but he also recognized the differences. John sang them a dirge and they didn't wail. Jesus piped them a merrier tune and they didn't dance. Neither way pleased the crowds. These two proverbial ways of putting it expressed the divergent styles of John and Jesus. "John came neither eating nor drinking, and they said, 'He is possessed by a demon!' The Son of Man came eating and drinking and they said, 'Look, he is a glutton and a drunkard, a friend of tax collectors and sinners!'" (Mt 11:18–19). Note that Jesus praised both ways as paths of righteousness, but no amount of puritanical piety can disguise the fact that the way of Jesus charts for us a merrier life.

Saturday of the
Second Week of Advent

Readings: Sirach 48:1–4, 9–11; Matthew 17:10–13

Orthodox Jews set a place for the prophet Elijah at the seder or Passover meal, in case he might return from the heavens the mysterious way he went (2 Kgs 2:1–13). Little children watch the cup of wine set at Elijah's place to see if he comes invisibly and disturbs it. Elijah hovers around much of the gospel narratives as well. Some eyewitnesses at the foot of the cross thought that the dying Jesus was calling on Elijah rather than "My God," in Aramaic, "*Eloi*" (Mk 15:35–36). The memory of Elijah, the quintessential prophet, is magnificently extolled by the late Jewish wisdom writer, Jesus ben Sirach (ca. 200 B.C.), and the thought that he might come again, mentioned in a late passage of the Old Testament (Mal 3:24–26), comes up for mention: "You are destined, it is written, in time to come/ to put an end to wrath before the day of the LORD,/ To turn back the hearts of fathers towards their sons,/ and to re-establish the tribes of Jacob" (Sir 48:10).

Does either the Old Testament or New Testament suggest a doctrine of reincarnation? No. But the New Testament descriptions of John the Baptist, and especially his rough clothing, indicate that he may well have consciously modeled himself on the fierce prophet Elijah, thought in popular Jewish lore to be coming again before the consummation of history. Jesus shared that notion with his contemporaries, but he also more importantly recognized the Elijah-like vocation of John: "I tell you that Elijah has already come, and they did not recognize him but did to him whatever they pleased." Different as Jesus and John the Baptist were in their proclamation of God's reign, Jesus recognized that they were headed for a similar fate: "So also will the the Son of Man suffer at their hands" (Mt 17:12).

All who follow Elijah and John and Jesus in the prophetic path can expect no better.

The
Third
Week
of
Advent

"...one among you whom you do not recognize...." (Jn 1:26)

Third Sunday of Advent (A)

Readings: Isaiah 35:1–6, 10; James 5:7–10;
Matthew 11:2–11

More Than a Prophet

New leaders in formerly Communist states and new leaders in the church are watched carefully in their early days in office for signals of what may be expected for the future. Is the new leader a champion of free-market economics and democratic political procedures or a throwback to the days of white-shirted, iron-eyed Brezhnev clones? Is the new pastor a shepherd with a sense that the sheep are not utterly stupid, or a walking advertisement for clerical clothes with ideas minted in the 1950s? The media in the United States want to know what the new Russian president thinks about NATO and nuclear disarmament. They want to know what the new pope thinks about the role of women in the church and the future of the celibate clergy. Smart Russian presidents and smart popes begin their terms of office with discreet silence, smiling a lot.

John the Baptist, jailed for his forthright denunciation of the infidelity of Herod Antipas to the covenant, wondered what to make of Jesus. Like the American press with regard to new Russian presidents and new popes, he watched every move of Jesus, trying to figure out its significance—at least as much as he could learn from prison. The gospel reading for this Sunday recounts the story of a man in jail, plagued with doubts and questions about the new leadership of his band of disciples. John the Baptist had foretold the coming of one "mightier than I" who would cleanse Israel of its iniquities: "His winnowing fan is in his hand" (Mt 3:11–12). But the one who came proved less stringent, perhaps, or less powerful than John had expected. Could this merciful preacher and miracle worker be the one expected?

Some said he was the Messiah, but what sort of messiah? A prophetic messiah modeled on Elijah would hardly socialize with tax collectors and prostitutes. A royal messiah modeled on David would hardly waste his political and military energies on preaching the beatitudes to the underclass in Galilee. A priestly messiah modeled on Aaron or Zadok should surely head for the Temple mount immediately and call the Roman-corrupted priesthood and the Sadducees to account. Jesus did not seem to fit into any of these patterns. "Are you the one who is to come, or should we look for another?" (Mt 11:3)

After the experience of the Babylonian exile on top of the Assyrian diaspora, the people of Yahweh saw not only their tribes dispersed but their land in ruins, desiccated and allowed to deteriorate. Their hopes for the messianic future involved not only a return to the land of Israel but also a restoration of its agricultural potential. The first reading for this Sunday, excerpted from Isaiah, celebrates that hoped-for future and encourages those who still must live in painful expectation: "Strengthen the hands that are feeble,/ make firm the knees that are weak,/ Say to those whose hearts are frightened:/ Be strong, fear not!" (Is 35:3–4).

The future restoration of Israel will also entail the future restoration of its handicapped: "Then will the eyes of the blind be opened,/ the ears of the deaf be cleared;/ Then will the lame leap like a stag,/ then the tongue of the dumb will sing" (Is 35:5–6). In responding to John the Baptist's query as to how the Messiah planned to clear the threshing floor of Israel, Jesus pointed to another and more merciful vision of the future, not unlike that of Isaiah: "The blind regain their sight, the lame walk, lepers are cleansed, the deaf hear, the dead are raised, and the poor have the good news proclaimed to them" (Mt 11:5).

The second reading, excerpted from the Letter of James, alludes to the coming of the Lord at the end of history in agricultural imagery; it attempts to encourage an early Christian community that was growing a bit restless with the indefinite postponement of their joy. But the agricultural imagery employed by James differs from the judgmental threshing-floor imagery of John the Baptist. For James, Jesus fulfills our expectations as a harvest, "the precious fruit of the earth" (Jas 5:7), fulfills the expectations of a patient farmer. John the Baptist learned to adjust his expectations. Like the farmer cited by James, he had to wait patiently. Watched pots don't boil and the crops in Israel needed both "the early and the late rains" (Jas 5:7) before the harvest. But the one who comes, in the words of Isaiah, still comes "with vindication" (Is 35:4). Vindication bodes well for the faithful but threatens the faithless. The first reading concentrates on the former, "those whom the LORD has ransomed" (Is 35:10).

Precisely because he was more than a prophet, John in prison could sense that his expectations were meeting their ironic fulfillment in Jesus. Jesus would clear the threshing floor by subjecting himself to the wind and fire of the cross. John preceded him in that as well, beheaded to please Herodias and her daughter (Mk 6:17–29). When Jesus came into the life of Israel as Messiah, he surprised those who had an agenda already set out for him. When he comes into our lives as well, he has surprises in store. "Blessed is the one who takes no offense at me" (Mt 11:6). John the Baptist made it over the stumbling block, and so can we.

Third Sunday of Advent (B)

Readings: Isaiah 61:1–2, 10–11; 1 Thessalonians 5:16–24; John 1:6–8, 19–28

Cause for Rejoicing

Pope John XXIII once alluded to "the prophets of doom" in Rome who tried to dissuade him from holding the Second Vatican Council. The descendants of those same prophets moved the late Karl Rahner to speak about the last years of his theological work as a time of winter in the church.

Developments in the church and in the world can often lead us to discouragement. But on this third Sunday of every Advent, the church bids us to rejoice, no matter how preoccupied we are with threats of ecclesial and secular doom. That is why this Sunday of Advent traditionally bears the Latin name *Gaudete*, from Paul's command to rejoice. The somber violet of Advent, in parishes with an extensive liturgical wardrobe, gives way to rose-colored vestments.

The first reading excerpted from the sixty-first chapter of Isaiah represents a dialogue between a prophet and the city of Jerusalem, the recipient of the prophet's good news. God's Spirit impels the prophet to announce especially good news for Jerusalem: its liberation from captivity and the advent of "a year of favor from the Lord" (Is 61:2). Jesus took this very text from Isaiah as the theme for his first sermon in Nazareth (Lk 4:18–19). Jerusalem, in response to the prophet, acknowledges that "God is the joy of my soul." Exuberantly, the Holy City compares itself to "a bride bedecked with her jewels" and also to a "bridegroom adorned with a diadem" (Is 61:10). No look-alike morning coats or tuxedos for the postexilic Jewish bridegroom!

Those who lead lives of selflessness, fulfilling themselves only by pointing to the way of Jesus, live in paradoxical joy. The nameless prophet whose call is narrated in the first reading, usually referred to as Third Isaiah by scholars, tells us that his prophetic calling brought him joy. It is never easy, in any day or age, "to bring glad tidings to the lowly,/ to heal the brokenhearted,/ to proclaim liberty to the captives/ and release to the prisoners" (Is 61:1). Ask any prison chaplain. But those who dedicate themselves to such obscure and difficult apostolates often turn out to be happier men and women than the superstars of ecclesiastical showbiz. Ask any cardinal.

Some of the earliest verses of John's Gospel that deal with

John the Baptist make up the gospel reading, presenting the Baptist as a witness "to testify to the light" (Jn 1:7). My master of novices, a man in whose presence I still feel a certain awe mixed with guilt for talking loudly in the corridors, always urged his charges in the Advent season not to "back off from the Baptist." The editors of the lectionary agree, drawing our attention in the second and third weeks of Advent to John the Baptist and his special role in the history of salvation.

In John's Gospel Jesus repeatedly uses the divine "I AM" to refer to himself, and that usage finally brings him to the cross, accused of blasphemy. John the Baptist, on the other hand, withdraws into the shadows in this gospel with his "I am not." When agents of the Sadducees, "priests and Levites" (Jn 1:19), came to interrogate him, he insisted on who he was not: not the Light, not the Messiah, not Elijah, not the Prophet like Moses. John might be analyzed today as someone with a very low sense of self-esteem. Who or what *was* John? Virtually nothing, he replied, quoting last week's first reading from Isaiah, nothing but "a voice of one crying out in the desert,/ 'Make straight the way of the Lord' " (Jn 1:23).

There is an ambiguity in that quotation from Isaiah. Does it mean "a voice shouting in the desert: Make straight the way of the Lord" or "a voice shouting: In the desert make straight the way of the Lord?" The Qumran sectarians of the late second Temple period read it the second way and invoked it as the constitution for their withdrawn existence in the wilderness of Judea, waiting for the Lord to come and purify the Temple in Jerusalem. John the Baptist, or at least the gospel writers, seem to have read the Isaiah text in a less sectarian mode. The voice may shout out in the wilderness, but those who hear it only come out to the wilderness to be urged to return to the cities and live different lives. John the Baptist withdrew into silence in the presence of the professionally religious, the religiously compromised.

The Pharisees, the pious laity who were the polar opposites of the compromised priestly class, picked up where the Sadducees rested their case. They wanted to know why John, if he was not inaugurating a messianic era or an apocalyptic or prophetic end of times, was performing ritual actions precisely suggestive of such a reality. Was he not drawing people to a ritual washing in the Jordan of the sort Ezekiel (36:25) and Zechariah (13:1) had pictured as symbolizing the purifying advent of God? "Why then do you baptize if you are not the Messiah or Elijah or the Prophet?" (Jn 1:25) John replied with his usual modesty, claiming comparatively little for his baptizing ministry: "I baptize with water; but there is one among you whom you do not recognize, the one who is coming after me whose sandal strap I am not worthy to untie" (Jn 1:26–27). The imagery is powerful. It is not hard to sympathize with the instinct of the Algerian independence leader, Ahmed Ben Bella, who abolished shoe shining in postcolonial Algeria in 1962. When John the Baptist defined himself as unworthy to undo the strap of the sandal of the one to come after him, it is hard not to be struck by his utter selflessness. It is indeed very tempting to back off from such selflessness.

Paul, another selfless prophet, bade the Thessalonians to live in joy as he did: "Rejoice always. Pray without ceasing. In all circumstance give thanks, for this is the will of God for you in Christ Jesus" (1 Thes 5:16–18). Prophets direct attention not to themselves, but to God. The prophet of Isaiah 61, Paul of Tarsus and John the Baptist all direct attention away from themselves to the joy of their souls: "The one who calls you is faithful" (1 Thes 5:24), as Paul writes. What better cause could we have for rejoicing than that?

Third Sunday of Advent (C)

Readings: Zephaniah 3:14–18; Philippians 4:4–7;
Luke 3:10–18

Nearness

New Yorkers share with Bostonians, Chicagoans and San Franciscans a certain fierce loyalty to the city of their birth or adoption. Many an actual denizen of the suburbs of those cities identifies himself or herself, when far from home, with the nearest metropolis, perhaps because the people of Katmandu and Ouagadougou have never heard of Short Hills, Scituate, Wilmette and Alameda.

Even in its period of late preexilic decline, the citizens of ancient Jerusalem also cultivated an intense loyalty to the city chosen by King David as the capital of united Judah and Israel. The prophet Zephaniah proved no exception, to judge from this joyful Advent Sunday's first reading. But Zephaniah knew Jerusalem well and did not ignore its failings as a Holy City. In the earlier part of this same chapter, Zephaniah reproached Jerusalem: "She hears no voice,/ accepts no correction;/ In the LORD she has not trusted,/ to her God she has not drawn near" (Zep 3:2). Once David had brought the Ark of the Covenant, Yahweh's throne or footstool, into the former Jebusite stronghold, Jerusalem centered itself on the invisible divine presence of the Lord. "The King of Israel, the LORD, is in your midst,/ you have no further misfortune to fear" (Zep 3:15). Even if the God of Israel kept his distance from any concretization in an image produced by human artistry, Yahweh stayed close to his people, dwelling invisibly in the Holy of Holies of the Temple on Mount Zion. "Yahweh your God...will dance with shouts of joy for you, as on a day of festival," in the translation of the New Jerusalem Bible (Zep 3:17). The New American Bible translates the same verse more prosaically, only allowing the Lord to sing.

The nearness of Yahweh to his people in Jerusalem preoccupied First Isaiah as well, the eighth-century B.C. prophet who foretold doom for Jerusalem's enemies and salvation for its children. The responsorial verses derive from Isaiah's song of thanksgiving for the intimacy Jerusalem enjoyed with the Almighty: "Shout with exultation, O city of Zion,/ for great in your midst/ is the Holy One of Israel!" (Is 12:6). Most ancient cities in the Middle East surrounded a temple; the difference between the Lord worshiped in Jerusalem and the divinities venerated in other capitals was that Yahweh scourged his people when they were faithless. The gods of Israel's neighbors, more patriotic than Yahweh, seldom rebuked their devotees.

The nearness of God in the new covenant took on a more temporal than geographical significance. Once God had entered into the human process in Jesus, he submitted to the bonds of historicity: past, present and future. Paul, writing to the Christians of Philippi, encouraged them to rejoice in the Lord always because "the Lord is near" (Phil 4:5). Like Paul, the Philippians had not known Jesus in his mortal existence. But they would know him when he came again in glory. The anxieties of the present in any generation yield to "the peace of God that surpasses all understanding" (Phil 4:7), when the faithful look forward in hope to the advent of the Lord. At least one strand of the New Testament tradition recognized that the messianic triumph of Jesus, begun in the resurrection, would not be complete until he comes in glory.

Lest we construe this Sunday's liturgy of the word as a mere eschatological pep talk, John the Baptist strides into center stage and directs our attention to the present as well as the future. Luke gives us three brief insights into what John the Baptist had to say to his contemporaries. Speaking not only to the affluent but also to the only moderately comfortable, John urged them to share what they had with the poor. To the illegitimately rich (at that time, tax collectors who might better be characterized as tax farmers, the highest bidders for government revenue-collecting jobs), John insisted that they "Stop collecting more than what is prescribed" (Lk 3:13). All the fun of tax collecting in Roman Palestine went up in smoke for any practitioner of that prosperous gouging who took John seriously. To the national security apparatus of Herodian Galilee or Roman-administered Judea, and especially those with qualms of conscience about their roles as enforcers of unpopular dictatorship, John offered the possibility of becoming decent policemen: "Do not practice extortion, do not falsely accuse anyone, and be satisfied with your wages" (Lk 3:14). John never shrank from controversy in his preaching.

John also looked forward to the future, as did his listeners. Although John had baptized the repentant with water, the one who was coming would "baptize you with the holy Spirit and in fire" (Lk 3:16). Not only would sins be washed away, but the coming Messiah would inaugurate a process of refining away the dross that lessens the value of our ore with the bellows of the Spirit and the fire of God's love. In another image closer to the experience of Jewish peasants, John compared the one who was coming to a wheat farmer who separates wheat from chaff by throwing the encumbered kernels into the wind, allowing the chaff to blow away and the kernels to fall to the threshing floor. Because the messianic Refiner and Winnower is near at hand, we begin to feel the heat of the fire and the blast of the wind.

> *Then cleansed be every breast from sin,*
> *Make straight the way for God within;*
> *And let us all our hearts prepare*
> *For Christ to come and enter there.*

Monday of the Third Week of Advent

Readings: Numbers 24:2–7, 15–17; Matthew 21:23–27

It wasn't easy for Balak to be king of Moab (in what is now Jordan) in the thirteenth century B.C., at the time the Israelites were passing through that territory on their Exodus from Egypt toward the Promised Land. Confronted with this massive and intimidating migration through his territory, Balak attempted to hire a professional curser, from what is now Syria, named Balaam, son of Beor, to lay a malediction on the Israelites. Balak should have looked more carefully into the religious proclivities of Balaam, whom the author of the Book of Numbers portrays as an agent not of Syrian deities but, at least on this occasion, of Yahweh, the God of Israel. Over and over again Balaam refused to curse Israel and, to add insult to injury, blessed them. The first reading features this blessing, and especially the words suggesting that the story of Balaam's blessing dates from the era of David's conquest of Moab (2 Sm 8:2): "I see him, though not now;/...A star shall advance from Jacob,/ and a staff shall arise from Israel" (Nm 24:17). In Israelite tradition Balaam was thought to have foreseen the rise of David to the kingship; early Christian tradition read the same text as pointing to the messianic advent of Jesus. The star followed by the Magi (Mt 2:2) may first have risen here.

The gospel reading returns to the figure of John the Baptist, albeit indirectly. Towards the end of his mortal ministry, after his triumphal entry into Jerusalem and his dramatic cleansing of the Temple, Jesus even dared to preach in those sacred precincts. The infuriated "chief priests and elders of the people" (Mt 21:23) challenged his authority for teaching in their religious bailiwick. Jesus agreed to tell them who had given him such authority, but first he wanted them to give their opinion on the authority by which John had baptized. "'Was it of heavenly or of human origin?'" (Mt 21:25). The priestly class had little regard for prophets of any sort. They probably regarded John the Baptist as an interloper in priestly affairs, not unlike the Qumran sectarians with whom he may once have had some connections, although Matthew tells us that some of the Sadducees, along with Pharisees, had approached John for baptism, only to be castigated as a "brood of vipers" (Mt 3:7).

To answer that John had baptized on divine authority laid them open to questioning as to why they had not abandoned their vipers' ways. To declare that John's baptism was based on authority that was "merely human" could have provoked a riot there and then in the Temple, because "the crowd...all regard John as a prophet" (Mt 21:26). Thus it was that the hierarchy came up with one of its very few admissions of ignorance: "We do not know" (Mt 21:27). Since they refused to answer his question about John's authority, Jesus refused to answer their question about his authority to preach in the Temple.

It's hard to challenge the authority of prophets like Balaam, John and Jesus, different as they are from each other, and hard to predict.

Tuesday of the Third Week of Advent

Readings: Zephaniah 3:1–2, 9–13; Matthew 21:28–32

Given the enthusiasm for Christianity of many varieties in much of Africa today, it seems incredible that so little was done to evangelize this part of the world before the early nineteenth century. The Portuguese *padroado* slowed down the Catholic evangelization of Africa more than it promoted it. Portuguese presence on the coasts of Africa from the fifteenth through the eighteenth centuries was identified with the exploitation of

the continent for slaves. Protestantism did little by way of evangelization of anyone but Europeans, wherever they lived, until
the Pietist movement of the eighteenth century helped
Protestants to overcome the odd idea that "idol worshipers"
anywhere in the world were being punished by God (see Rom
1:18–23) for rejecting the message of the Apostles.

The prophet Zephaniah, proclaiming God's message in
Jerusalem in the seventh century B.C., blasted the Judean capital for its faithlessness and suggested that Gentiles might yet
prove worthier of hearing God's word. "From beyond the rivers
of Ethiopia/ and as far as the recesses of the North,/ they shall
bring me offerings" (Zep 3:10). Like the African Christians of
today who could put to shame the insouciant Christians of so
much of the "developed" world, the Gentiles of Africa struck
the prophet Zephaniah as likely candidates, along with a
saved remnant in Jerusalem, to be "a people humble and
lowly" (Zep 3:12).

The gospel passage continues yesterday's confrontation
between Jesus and the Jerusalem priesthood on the subject of
John the Baptist. Jesus proposed a parable of two sons, one of
them professing obedience to his father but not carrying it out,
and the other, at first refusing obedience, but eventually carrying out the work in the vineyard, as the father had commanded. Which son obeyed the father? The priests fell into the
trap and, naturally, picked the second son. Jesus then explained
who the two sons of his parable were. "Tax collectors and prostitutes are entering the kingdom of God before you" (Mt 21:31),
these sinners having responded to John's preaching despite
their previous disobedience to the Law. As for the officiants of
Temple piety, "even when you saw that, you did not later
change your mind and believe him" (Mt 21:32).

The openness of both John the Baptist and Jesus to tax
collectors and prostitutes, and the response of these unlikely

converts to both John and Jesus, eventually prepared the early church to take seriously the possibility, adumbrated in Zephaniah, that "Gentile sinners" might also be welcome among the new people of God.

Wednesday of the Third Week of Advent

Readings: Isaiah 45:6–8, 18, 21–25; Luke 7:18–23

J. Robert Oppenheimer, on witnessing, in 1945, the first atomic blast in the New Mexico desert, thought of the famous words of the god Vishnu, as put into the mouth of his *avatara* Krishna in the *Bhagavad Gita*: "I am become death, the shatterer of the worlds." Unlike the Lord Vishnu, the Lord of Israel would never say such a thing, but in Second Isaiah he does declare that "I form the light, and create the darkness,/ I make well-being and create woe;/ I, the LORD, do all these things" (Is 45:7). In the first chapter of Genesis, "God looked at everything he had made, and he found it very good" (Gn 1:31). It may be that the human authors and editors of the first chapter of Genesis were reacting against cosmic dualism, the later Persian tendency to divide all reality into two, the creation of a good

Lord and the creation of an evil Spirit. Prophets like Second Isaiah may have introduced some of this cosmic dualism into Judaism after the Persian liberation of the Jews from Babylon, especially the notion that some things are created evil.

Although it is hard to tell from the edited version of chapter 45 of Isaiah in today's first reading, God's words in it were addressed to a non-Jew, the Persian world-conqueror and cosmic dualist Cyrus the Great. But, for all the fact that Second Isaiah called Cyrus God's "anointed" (i.e., messiah: Is 45:1), Yahweh insisted on the absolute divine singularity, an issue not so clear in earlier passages of the Hebrew Bible: "I am the LORD, and there is no other" (Is 45:18). Not only is Yahweh one and one alone, but his reign extends to all humankind: "To me every knee shall bend;/ by me every tongue shall swear" (Is 45:23).

John the Baptist, imprisoned, wondered whether he had done the right thing in handing his disciples over to such a mild-mannered figure as Jesus. Through two of his disciples, people he had undoubtedly prepared for the coming of one whose "winnowing fan is in his hand" (Lk 3:17), John questioned Jesus about his identity. "Are you the one who is to come, or should we look for another?" (Lk 7:19). The evangelist indicates that, far from winnowing, gathering and burning, Jesus at that time "cured many of their diseases, sufferings, and evil spirits; he also granted sight to many who were blind" (Lk 7:21). Jesus told John's envoys to report to him that they had seen him do such works of mercy, including not only physical miracles but a major social and religious miracle as well: "...the poor have the good news proclaimed to them" (Lk 7:22). In the darkness of his prison cell and the darkness of his soul, John caught some glimmer of the coming dawn. "Blessed is the one who takes no offense at me" (Lk 7:23).

Thursday of the
Third Week of Advent

Readings: Isaiah 54:1–10; Lk. 7:24–30

Marriage is serious business, although all too many Americans do not realize this, to judge from the divorce rate. The ancient Israelites saw it as the central link between generations, making possible the promise to Abraham that "your own issue shall be your heir" (Gn 15:4). In the Book of Ruth–anti-Ezra propaganda of the postexilic era, very likely, demonstrating that Gentile wives *can* continue the line of Israel and even prepare the way for King David–the Moabitess Ruth, widow of a Bethlehemite, found her "redeemer" from the status of childless widowhood in Boaz, her husband's kinsman (Ru 4:10–17). The first reading today returns to this image of redeeming a widow or spinster through marriage, but the bridegroom in this reading is Yahweh, redeemer of Israel from the barrenness of exile. "For he who has become your husband is your Maker;/ his name is the LORD of hosts;/ Your redeemer is the Holy One of Israel,/ called God of all the earth" (Is 54: 5).

Today's gospel continues from yesterday's, also concentrating on the relationship between Jesus and John the Baptist. Jesus said of John the Baptist that he was something more than a prophet. Quoting the prophecy of Malachi, Jesus identifies John as "my messenger" (Mal 3:1), that figure of the end of times who would prepare for what and who would follow. Jesus himself would eventually reveal his identity as "the way and the truth and the life" (Jn 14:6) in John's Gospel, much more than a messenger. A prophet or a messenger cannot save, only prophesy or deliver the message. Jesus came as what prophet and messenger glimpsed partially, the Redeemer of all our widowhood, all our barrenness.

Friday of the Third Week of Advent

Readings: Isaiah 56:1–3, 6–8; John 5:33–36

As if life were not already hard enough for eunuchs, the editors of the lectionary have cut them out of the first reading of this Advent weekday as well, and in the process the editors have lost some of the text's meaning. Third Isaiah begins his contribution to scripture with the hope that those normally excluded from the first Temple—non-Jewish foreigners and eunuchs, those who cannot continue the progeny of Israel—will be admitted to the second Temple. "Let not the foreigner say,/ when he would join himself to the LORD,/ 'The LORD will surely exclude me from his people';/ Nor let the eunuch say,/ 'See, I am a dry tree' " (Is 56:3). That hope was at least partly fulfilled with the construction of the Court of the Gentiles in Herod's reconstruction (almost total) of the second Temple. The Acts of the Apostles indicates that an Ethiopian eunuch, presumably a Jew by birth or conversion and serving as treasurer to the queen mother (Kandake) of ancient Nubia in what is now northern Sudan, "had come to Jerusalem to worship" (Acts 8:27), so the ban on noncontributors to the population of Israel visiting the Temple had obviously been lifted by the time of Jesus.

The final gospel passage in a series about John the Baptist that began a week ago yesterday comes today from John's Gospel. Queried about his authority to heal on the sabbath, Jesus claimed for himself the prerogative of God to violate human regulations about the weekly day of rest. He then returned to the law-court imagery of John's Gospel, citing God as his chief character witness (Jn 5:33). With such a divine witness, Jesus hardly needed even as upstanding a figure as John the Baptist to testify for him, but Jesus paid tribute nonetheless to his forerunner. "He was a burning and shining lamp, and for a while you were content to rejoice in his light" (Jn 5:35). But the brightness of God's testimony in the miracles Jesus performed outshone the lamp of John. "But I have testimony greater than John's. The works that the Father gave me to accomplish" (Jn 5:36). There is something a little sad in this gospel passage, the subordination of the valiant Baptist to the one who came after him. John the Baptist had prepared himself for this, according to John's Gospel: "He must increase; I must decrease" (Jn 3:30).

NOTE

There is no *Saturday of the Third Week of Advent* because, by that time in every construction of the calendar–and often earlier–the 'late Advent weekdays' have begun, namely, December 17–24. Reflections on those days' liturgical readings follow the *Fourth Sunday of Advent*.

The
Fourth
Week
of
Advent

"...the virgin shall be with child and bear a son...." (Mt 1:23)

Fourth Sunday of Advent (A)

Readings: Isaiah 7:10–14; Romans 1:1–7;
Matthew 1:18–24

Dealing with Doubts

Americans go through various trends in naming their children. Whereas many Europeans until a generation ago loyally named firstborn sons after the paternal grandfather, firstborn daughters after the paternal grandmother second-born sons after the maternal grandfather and second-born daughters after the maternal grandmother, Americans often named their children after themselves. Thus came to birth a generation of Sonnies, Juniors, Chips, Buddies, Babes and Sisses. Nowadays all too many Americans name their children after actors like Ryan O'Neal or geographical features of Ireland like Kerry and the River Shannon, or nothing at all, only a charming sound.

Naming in ancient times said something about the parents' hopes for the newborn, or even God's hopes for the newborn, as revealed through a prophet. Yahweh, who made Isaiah a prophet, insisted that peculiar names mark Isaiah's children out as signs of what would come of the Syro-Ephraimite war in the last third of the eighth century B.C. Thus little *Shear-jashub* ("A remnant will return," Is 7:3) reminded the fearful king of Judah at the time that God would rescue at least *some* of the besieged Judeans from their Syrian and northern-kingdom enemies. *Maher-shalal-hash-baz* ("Quick spoils; speedy plunder," Is 8:1)–saddled with a name like that must have made him regret his father's prophetic work–symbolized the eventual defeat of Judah's foes, an eventuality the child may have celebrated by changing his name.

Between these two prophetic children Isaiah or the fearful king (the text is unclear) would father a child to be named Immanuel, "With us is God" (Is 7:14). Who is the mother of this child? The Hebrew text of Isaiah assures us that she is still young at the time of the prophetic naming of her future child; the Alexandrian Jewish translation of the passage into Greek suggested that she was a virgin, as yet unmarried. The point of the text, in its original setting, is that this young woman's eventual child will reach what later times would call the age of reason before "the land of those two kings whom you dread shall be deserted" (Is 7:16). Victory was coming, but not immediately. Meanwhile, keep faith!

The evangelist Matthew, quoting the Greek translation of the Old Testament, saw the birth of Immanuel in Isaiah's prophecy as a foreshadowing of the virginal conception of Jesus. But the mother of Jesus broke all expectations, someone quite different from Isaiah's "prophetess" (Is 8:3). The prophetic Spirit that filled her brought to birth not only what Paul, in the second reading, calls one "descended from David according to the flesh" but also one "established as Son of God in power" (Rom 1:3–4). They named this child not Immanuel but Jesus, the Greek form of *Yeshua* (a variant of *Joshua*), "because he will save his people from their sins" (Mt 1:21). Not even Isaiah could have expected that.

Why did the rabbis in Alexandria in the third century B.C., translating the Book of Isaiah into Greek, render the Hebrew word *'almah* (young woman) by the Greek word *parthenos* (virgin)? We shall probably never know. In the original Hebrew text, Isaiah offered to King Ahaz, in a quandary over what to do between the importunities of the Assyrians and the attack of Syria in alliance with the northern kingdom (Israel), a sign of hope. The new child, to be born either in the prophet's household or in the king's, would bear a name signifiying that, no matter how bad military and political affairs seem to be going, God is still with us. Before that child matured, the troubles besetting Ahaz would be relieved.

In the long run, Ahaz and everyone else in the Davidic dynasty were disappointed. The Assyrians overwhelmed the northern kingdom in 721 B.C., and the Chaldeans devastated Jerusalem in what remained of the southern kingdom in 587 B.C. Like every other prophecy of future happiness, the Immanuel text still looked forward in hope. Matthew, after his genealogy of the Israelite and Davidic ancestors of Jesus (Mt 1:1–17), offers us, in the narrative of the birth of this last and greatest king in the Davidic line, the consolation that Isaiah's words of comfort finally had their day. "All this took place to fulfill what the Lord had said through the prophet" (Mt 1:22).

The doubts of John the Baptist, confronted in last Sunday's gospel with a messiah less militant than he had hoped for, pale in comparison with the doubts faced by Joseph, "a righteous man" (Mt 1:19). Were Joseph to define his uprightness by the standards of the Torah, he should expose his pregnant fiancee to the ordeal described by the Book of Numbers (5:5–31). But Joseph's uprightness derived not from the Law, but from uttermost faith in God: "It is through the holy Spirit that this child has been conceived in her" (Mt 1:20). Not only is a new law in prospect but a new creation, the birth of a new Adam from the womb of a new and innocent Eve.

St. Paul opened his Letter to the Romans with a trumpet blast, asserting his rights as "an apostle...set apart for the gospel of God which he promised previously through his prophets" (Rom 1:1–2). The gospel of God–good news for those in doubts about matters of state or family affairs or anything in between–comes to us through people very like ourselves, men and women who have suffered doubts of their own. Their faith–fidelity to God who has first kept faith with us–brings about something utterly new and utterly different in the history of humankind, the new humanity that is Jesus.

Fourth Sunday of Advent (B)

Readings: 2 Samuel 7:1–5, 8–11, 16;
Romans 16:25–27; Luke 1:26–38

Master of the Household

"They don't build houses the way they used to," complains the owner of a modern house, appalled by defects in its construction. Real estate agents for older dwellings join in the chorus. But the psalmist cautions that "Unless the LORD build the house,/ they labor in vain who build it" (Ps 127:1), whether the construction be ancient or modern. What can be said of houses applies to households as well: The historical decline of dynasties provides the stuff of history. The Hapsburgs, the Hohenzollerns, the Mountbatten-Windsors, the Roosevelts, the Kennedys, the Nehru-Gandhis, the Pahlavis and the Bhuttos all exemplify this generalization. On the fourth Sunday of Advent the readings turn our attention to house building and dynasty building.

David the king had hoped to build a sacred house for Yahweh, but the prophet Nathan intervened. Solomon eventually built the Temple, but in a sense what he built was only a chapel appended to the much more grandiose royal precincts. In dealing with David, Yahweh rejected containment in human structures and insisted, in its stead, on building a house for David. The responsorial psalm preserves an ancient poetic version of the covenant God made with David, a covenant in which God adopts the king in Jerusalem as a son. "I have made a covenant with my chosen one,/ I have sworn to David my servant:/ Forever will I confirm your posterity/ and establish your throne for all generations" (Ps 89:4–5). Despite all these divine promises, David's royal lineage lasted only four centuries on the throne in Jerusalem, collapsing with the Chaldean conquest and the beginning of the Babylonian exile.

In making David Yahweh's anointed, the king of Judah and Israel, God had taken all the initiative. What was David before God chose him? Virtually nothing: a shepherd boy. "'I...took you from the pasture and from the care of the flock to be commander of my people Israel'" (2 Sm 7:8). The judge and prophet Samuel, acting on God's behalf, had exalted the lowly and brought down the mighty from their thrones. When David, shepherd boy turned king, took on airs and began to behave like every other despot in the ancient Middle East, Nathan would remind him that the divine law against murder and adultery applied to kings as well. David was a triumph of God's sovereign choosing, not an accomplishment of the family of Jesse or the tribe of Judah.

The first reading for this final Sunday of Advent narrates how Yahweh refused David's offer of a house and assured the king that God would prefer to establish a dynasty for David and his descendants: "'Your house and your kingdom shall endure forever before me; your throne shall stand firm forever'" (2 Sm 7:16). The absolute and unconditional quality of this promise perturbed the faith of later generations in Israel, and especially the faith of those postexilic Jews whose hopes for a revival of the Davidic royal line met constant frustration. God eventually fulfilled his promise to David, but in a manner that neither the warrior king nor any of his immediate successors would have suspected.

Luke's account of the annunciation stresses the Davidic and

royal descent of the child to be born of Mary. Even if David's house did not last forever, in Jesus it received a new beginning: "Of his kingdom there will be no end" (Lk 1:33). No worldly Solomon will succeed this new David. The Spirit of God's holiness enters and makes this a royal house. If the Davidic kings were adoptive "sons of God," the true Son of God will be born of Mary! But the best promise is kept for the end. The child to be born of Mary would be not an aspiring temple builder but a new Temple, himself the dwelling place of God: "The holy Spirit will come upon you, and the power of the Most High will overshadow you. Therefore, the child to be born will be called holy, the Son of God" (Lk 1:35). Both the kingship and the Temple came to the house of David in a woman named Mary, a virtual nobody from "a town of Galilee called Nazareth" (Lk 1:26). Thus has God "thrown down the rulers from their thrones/ but lifted up the lowly" (Lk 1:52).

Breaking out of the household of David and the descent of Jacob, the child born of Mary was one of us and yet not one of us. As such, he rules over the house of Jacob *and* over the house of Esau forever. Paul notes in the final doxology of the Epistle to the Romans that Jesus is the Messiah appointed by God, not only to rule the Jews but also "made known to all nations to bring about the obedience of faith" (Rom 16:26). This extension of divine salvation and messianic rule not only to the Jews but also to Gentiles is "the mystery kept secret for long ages but now manifested" (Rom 16:25–26). Here is a household worthy of the God who created everything and everyone, a household without closed doors or barred entrances.

Advent and Christmas come at the end of the old civil year, another year in which we have come to recognize our old incivilities, our old proclivities, our old orneriness. But before the old year runs out, the church surprises us with a new liturgical year, a new start on the reality God deals us. In the new year, God will surprise us with many more new things, as he surprised the Virgin of Nazareth. What should be our response? The same as hers: "I am the handmaid of the Lord. May it be done to me according to your word" (Lk 1:38). It is difficult to say those words and mean them. But that is the vocation of every Christian, indeed, of every human being. We have to let God be God and let ourselves be what we were created to be: the work of God's hand, the recipients of his creative love, the servants of the Lord. If we surrender ourselves to this reality, we will come to some glimpse of the very selfhood of God. Then the Holy Spirit may come upon us and the power of the Most High may overshadow us. And Jesus can be born again.

Fourth Sunday of Advent (C)

Readings: Micah 5:1–4; Hebrews 10:5–10; Luke 1:39–45

She Who Believed

Saint Edith Stein, the philosopher and Carmelite, entered into the passion and death of Christ along with millions of Jews slaughtered by the Nazi death machine. Very much a modern professional woman, Stein had suffered misogynistic

"...the angel of the Lord appeared to him in a dream...." (Mt 1:20)

rejection from many of her academic colleagues in the years before she entered Carmel. But the life of a contemplative nun did not offer her an escape from reality, as events proved. Rather, the simplification that such a life makes possible prepared her to face the ultimate in human hatred for a fellow human being: the Holocaust. In canonizing Edith Stein, Pope John Paul II has offered her to the modern world, male and female, as a model of the truly human, filled with faith and hope and love in the face of horror. On this final Sunday of Advent, the church presents us with models of true humanity: the little town of Bethlehem, two pregnant women, Jesus coming into the world. The frivolity of the coming Christmas season must not distract us from the reality faced by each.

The passage from the prophecy of Micah (eighth century B.C.) excerpted in the first reading makes more sense in its larger context. In chapter 4 of Micah, Jerusalem is extolled in idealizing terms, its future better than its past: "In days to come/ the mount of the LORD's house/ Shall be established higher than the mountains..../From Zion shall go forth instruction,/ and the word of the LORD from Jerusalem" (Mi 4:1, 2). But the end of the chapter brings in a more somber picture of Jerusalem besieged by its enemies: "For now shall you go forth from the city/ and dwell in the fields;/ To Babylon shall you go,/ there shall you be rescued" (Mi 4:10). This Sunday's reading contrasts Bethlehem, a village five miles from Jerusalem and the native place of King David, with the citadel David built at Jerusalem. Just as David, the youngest son of Jesse, surprised his clan with his military prowess and royal destiny, a new David yet to be born would come to birth in Bethlehem to rescue the children of Israel from foreign domination: "He shall stand firm and shepherd his flock/ by the strength of the LORD" (Mi 5:3). Bethlehem, small as it was, could with God's help do the impossible again.

Micah lamented the decline of the Davidic kingdom in which he lived, its falling away from the standards of fidelity to Yahweh set by King David. Yearning for a new David, Micah fantasized that Bethlehem, the monarch's humble place of origin, might bring forth another just ruler for the chosen people. The mother of that future king—Bethlehem itself or a particular woman in the Davidic line—would experience a difficult time while awaiting the Messiah's birth. But "when she who is to give birth has borne," then the prophet hoped that "the rest of his brethren shall return to the children of Israel" (Mi 5:2). The present distress of Yahweh's people, like labor pains, would eventually result in joy.

The two pregnant women in the gospel reading, Mary and Elizabeth, recognized in each other signs from God. The angel Gabriel, in the passage just before this excerpt, had offered Mary a lesser parallel to her own virginal conception of Jesus: "And behold, Elizabeth your relative, has also conceived a son in her old age, and this is the sixth month for her who was called barren; for nothing will be impossible for God" (Lk 1:36). Elizabeth in her turn sensed in the movement of the child in her womb on Mary's arrival that something extraordinary was happening. "How does this happen to me, that the mother of my Lord should come to me?" (Lk 1:43).

Each of these pregnant women experienced in herself the possibility of the impossible. The visitation of Mary to Elizabeth turned out to be a divine visitation, the Ark of God bringing not terror but blessing as it did to the house of Obededom the Gittite (1 Sm 6:9–11). Unlike Sarah, who had laughed at the notion that she could conceive in her old age and bear a child to Abraham (Gn 18:12), and unlike Zechariah, her husband, who had been struck dumb for questioning God's power in this matter (Lk 1:18–20), Elizabeth gave thanks to God and trusted in his providence: "So has the Lord done for me at a time when he has seen fit to take away my disgrace before others" (Lk 1:25). Mary, for her part, deserved to be acclaimed by Elizabeth as she "who believed that what was spoken to you by the Lord would be fulfilled" (Lk 1:45).

Later in the Gospel of Luke we read how Jesus responded to the woman who uttered a blessing on "the womb that carried you and the breasts at which you nursed." Jesus insisted that physical maternity merited much less praise than spiritual: "Rather, blessed are those who hear the word of God and observe it" (Lk 11:27–28). Mary's trust in God marked her from the moment of her entry into our history until her exit: the handmaid of the Lord (Lk 1:38) who was eventually to become the mother of God, the mother of the Beloved Disciple (Jn 19:26–27). Hearing the word of God, allowing it to come to birth in a fruitful life, characterized both Elizabeth and Mary. The Magnificat, the immediate sequel to this gospel passage, celebrates the wonders of God's graciousness in the lives not only of these two women but of all for whom "the Mighty One has done great things" (Lk 1:49).

Jesus, as much God's Son as Mary's, is said by the author of the Epistle to the Hebrews to have come into the world with the words of Psalm 40 on his lips: " 'As is written of me in the scroll,/ Behold, I come to do your will, O God' " (Heb 10:7, quoting Ps 40:8–9). In Jesus a faithful God and a faith-filled humanity met. As the son of Mary, Jesus learned faith from his parents, and especially from the woman praised by Elizabeth as one who believed that the Lord's words to her would be fulfilled. At Christmas time many Americans come home, not only to their parents but also to their churches; they may not stay home very long with either their parents or their churches. But Christmas is no time for either parents or church to berate them. Welcome them as Elizabeth welcomed Mary. God's Spirit may stir new life within them.

December 17

Readings: Genesis 49:2, 8–10; Matthew 1:1–17

We all have skeletons in our closets. Matthew's Gospel doesn't hide the oddities, eccentricities and angularities in the ancestral lineage of Jesus. If anything, Matthew deliberately points them out, to give hope to those of us who don't fit into ordinary categories. First of all, Jesus, like King David, was descended from Judah, one of the twelve sons of Jacob or Israel. The first reading, excerpted from the poetic last will and testament of Jacob, contains some of what Jacob predicted for Judah: "Judah, like a lion's whelp,/ you have grown up on prey, my son./ He crouches like a lion recumbent,/ the king of beasts–who would dare rouse him?" (Gn 49:9). The kingship that David seized from Saul fulfills this prediction better than the kingship on the cross of the Lamb of God.

But another and less reputable aspect of Judah's career plays into the genealogy of Jesus, according to Matthew. "Judah was the father of Perez and Zerah, whose mother was Tamar" (Mt 1:3). Judah was not young when he fathered twins with Tamar, who had been his daughter-in-law, the wife of his son Er. Er died young and childless, punished by God for offenses unspecified, and his brother Onan refused to beget a child in his place with Tamar, rebelling against what came to be called the law of levirate (Dt 25:5). This act of disobedience cost him his life as well. Judah let the matter rest at that and did not provide his widowed daughter-in-law with the third son when he grew up, even though he had promised to do so. Tamar took matters into her own hands and, disguised as a prostitute, seduced her father-in-law, became pregnant by him and gave birth to twins (Gn 38:1–30). How's that for a nice story about your ancestry?

Matthew continues in this direction, citing as well, among the forbearers of Jesus, Rahab, the heroic prostitute of Jericho (Jos 2:1–21; 6:22–25), and Ruth, the Moabite widow of a childless Jew who finagled Boaz into a levirate marriage of sorts (Ru 1–4). Last, but not least, Bathsheba, the almost unmentionable woman who "had been the wife of Uriah" (Mt 1:6), enters the lineage, mistress and later spouse of David and mother of Solomon (2 Sm 11:1–27). What all four of these women, the only ones cited in the patrilineal genealogy of Jesus, had in common was the unusual (to put it mildly) nature of their continuing the line of Judah. Furthermore, there is something Gentile about all four: the first disguised as a Canaanite temple prostitute, the second a definitely Gentile prostitute of philo-Israelite political sympathies, the third a Moabite widow and convert, the fourth married to an upright Hittite Gentile whom she and David cuckolded and then liquidated. God writes straight with the crooked lines of our family history.

Into the line of Judah, the ancestor of Joseph who married Mary, was born a child whom Joseph never begot but whom he fathered nonetheless. "Jacob [was] the father of Joseph, the husband of Mary. Of her was born Jesus who is called the Messiah" (Mt 1:16). The patrilineal genealogy builds up to nothing. Even if he was adopted by Joseph, Jesus did not physically belong to the house of David, the house of Jacob, the house of Abraham in any limiting sense. The new creation began in him, with God's mysterious wisdom overcoming human fallibility.

The first of the late Advent "O-antiphons," used in the

Prayer of the Church before and after the Magnificat of Evening Prayer, suitably dwells today on that inscrutable divine wisdom: "O Wisdom of our God Most High, guiding creation with power and love: teach us to walk in the paths of knowledge."

December 18

Readings: Jeremiah 23:5–8; Matthew 1:18–24

There are spelling checkers on computers that know jeremiads but not Jeremiah, who gave them their origin. Jeremiah was called by God to deliver a lot of bad news to the patriots of Jerusalem in the decades leading up to the Babylonian conquest and the consequent exile; he engaged in eloquent jeremiads. The first reading today offers us a breather from his usual lament. Dating at least partly from those last days before the exile, when Zedekiah, uncle of the last legitimate ruler of Jerusalem (Jehoiachin) and puppet of the Babylonians for more than ten years (597–586 B.C.), was presiding over the dissolution of Jerusalem, the prophecy looks forward to a real king whose life will epitomize what Zedekiah's name only means: "'The LORD our justice'" (Jer 23:6). Kingship in the de facto house of David turned out to be a failed experiment in governance, as Samuel had predicted (1 Sm 8:10–18). But hope for the fulfillment of God's unconditional covenant with David lived on in Jewish hearts: "Behold, the days are coming, says the LORD,/ when I will raise up a righteous shoot to David" (Jer 23:5).

Matthew's Gospel, after tracing the flawed human genealogy of Jesus, presents us with the birth of that "righteous shoot" in apparently the most unrighteous circumstances. What we used to call an unwed mother, nearly repudiated by her fiancé for what seemed like premarital unchastity, revived eternally the royal throne of David. All those unusual female forbears of Jesus in yesterday's gospel passage prepare us for the most extraordinary one of all, the virgin Mary. The prophet Nathan, on God's behalf, had assured the warrior-king David that God would build him an eternal house: "Your house and your kingdom shall endure forever before me; your throne shall stand firm forever" (2 Sm 7:16). And yet, over the centuries that had passed since the Babylonian exile, no descendant of David had reigned over God's people. Finally, the line of David was to be revived, but in the most embarrassing circumstances. Joseph, "a righteous man" and yet, with Christlike inconsistency (Jn 8:1–11), "unwilling to expose her to shame" (Mt 1:19), came under the impetus of an angelic dream visitation to see Mary's situation differently. "It is through the holy Spirit that this child has been conceived in her. She will bear a son and you are to name him Jesus, because he will save his people from their sins" (Mt 1:20–21). Such naming of a child not his own legitimized him in Israelite law. The uprightness of Joseph was not that of little minds.

The O-antiphon for this late Advent weekday addresses God by the royal title usually translated as "Lord," *Adonai,* the Hebrew avoidance-name for Yahweh. Yahweh, who had ruled Israel through Moses, Joshua and the judges before Saul's and

David's reigns, is asked to come and rule his people once again: "O Leader of ancient Israel, giver of the Law of Moses on Sinai, rescue us with your mighty power."

December 19

Readings: Judges 13:2–7, 24–25; Luke 1:5–25

Anthropologists in some future century may wonder why many young people in the late second-and early third-millennium-A.D. United States, while asserting their independence of parental norms, express their "individualism" by conforming to media-generated fashions. Thus, the future scholars will observe, young Americans at that time wore baseball caps (backwards) as well as oversized, baggy blue jeans and expensive shirts emblazoned with advertisements for their manufacturers. Professional sportsmen shaved their heads and many young people, male and female, felt the need to wear earrings, if not other, more distracting facial metal.

These curious American rites of self-mutilation or uniform dressing, grist for the mill of future anthropologists, bear some kinship to the nazirite vows of the ancient Jews, the consecration either for life or for a limited time, of a Jewish man or woman to certain notable practices of asceticism:

"When a man (or a woman) solemnly takes the nazirite vow,...he shall abstain from wine and strong drink...[and] no razor shall touch his hair" (Nm 6:2, 5). Samson, as the first reading narrates, and also Samuel provide examples of this in the Old Testament, and each was so dedicated as a thanksgiving offering by previously childless parents. An angel tells the mother-to-be of Samson that "this boy is to be consecrated to God from the womb" (Jgs 13:5).

The first reading prepares us for Luke's account of the annunciation to Zechariah, a childless priest of the Temple in Jerusalem, that his aging wife Elizabeth will at last give birth to a son, John the Baptist, who is to be consecrated as a nazirite. "He will drink neither wine nor strong drink. He will be filled with the holy Spirit even from his mother's womb" (Lk 1:15). Luke's interest in the vocation of John the Baptist may have arisen from some little understood controversy in the first decades of the church between disciples of John the Baptist (including, possibly, Apollos) and disciples of Jesus (see Acts 18:24–19:7; also 1 Cor 1:12; 3:1–9). Both Luke and John found it important to distinguish between the Way of the Lord according to John and the Way of the Lord according to Jesus, showing the superiority of the second. That superiority is acted out, as it were, in the contrasting angelic annunciations to Zechariah and Mary. Zechariah doubted the angelic annunciation on the basis of his own and his wife's advanced age. Mary only questioned how the conception of Jesus could occur without her having a husband. Zechariah is struck with muteness for a time, "until the day these things take place, because you did not believe my words" (Lk 1:20). In his muteness he still was able to beget with Elizabeth the voice that cried in the wilderness.

The O-antiphon for this day looks forward to the flowering of the long barren royal family tree of Jesse, the father of King

David: "O Flower of Jesse's stem, come sign of God's love for all his people: save us without delay!"

December 20

Readings: Isaiah 7:10–14; Luke 1:26–38

The central paradox of Christianity, the triumph over evil effected on the cross, begins its history in the apparent disgrace of a girl from the village of Nazareth in Galilee, "a virgin betrothed to a man named Joseph, of the house of David" (Lk 1:27). The new house of David, begun by angelic annunciation in Nazareth, was accomplished by God's sovereign initiative working with most unlikely material: a simple adolescent girl engaged to be married to a man named Joseph. The virginal conception and birth of Jesus make no sense in biological terms; we know that the sex of a child is determined by the chromosomal input of the father. And yet the New Testament, in the different testimonies of Matthew and Luke, assures us that Jesus had no human father. Matthew certainly and Luke probably looked to Isaiah's reassurance of the weak King Ahaz in Jerusalem with a prophecy of the birth of the child to be named Immanuel ("God is with us") for a parallel, but the virgin (*parthenos*) of the Greek translation of the Old

Testament is merely a young woman (*'almah*) in the Hebrew original, and the virgin birth in both Matthew's and Luke's infancy narratives asserts much more than does Isaiah.

The work of God transcended purely human generation, amazing as it is. The conception and birth of any child is astounding, the more one knows of the process. But the conception and birth of this child was a new creation, a new beginning not only of the house of David but of the house of Adam, humanity. The Qur'an puts it quite vividly:

> "Lord," [Mariyam] said, "how can I bear a child when no man has touched me?" [The angel] replied: "Even thus. God creates whom He will. When He decrees a thing He need only say: 'Be,' and it is."
>
> Qur'an 3:47

We have little to say of importance about the wonder of the virginal conception of Jesus in the womb of Mary. In some sense, that is the very importance of the virginal conception of Jesus: we have little to say. We have no power to create ourselves, no power to save ourselves. Every addict knows this in an experiential sense, and once we have come to recognize in the depth of our hearts that we live in utter dependence on a creative and rescuing God, we can begin to come to terms with the wonder of the virginal conception and birth of Jesus. If God resembled you and me, God would finally be unbelievable, unworthy of trust, unreliable. But God is different and God's ways are not merely human ways. The virginal conception of Jesus, like his bodily resurrection, stand as signs for us that God can create again and again. There is a chance for you and me as well, that God can re-create us, make us new.

The O-antiphon recognizes in Jesus the true majesty of the

house of David, symbolized in Isaiah by "the key of the House of David" entrusted to the master of the royal palace (Is. 22:22). In Jesus we have as well the master of the palace of God: "O Key of David, come and open the gates of God's eternal kingdom, freeing the prisoners of darkness!"

December 21

Readings: Song of Songs 2:8–14 or Zephaniah 3:14–18;
Luke 1:39–45

One experience reserved to women that a man can share only vicariously is pregnancy. In many traditional societies, men might not enter into a room where a woman is giving birth. Nowadays, many husbands share with their wives not only the moment of birth but even the exercises and other preparations over many months before the big day. But still, the man cannot feel the baby inside himself; he cannot know in the same way a woman can the pains of labor and the joy of giving birth.

Luke's Gospel, attempting to summarize symbolically the deepest significance of the life, death and resurrection of Jesus in terms of his infancy, draws a particularly intriguing picture of the relationship between John the Baptist and Jesus in terms of the relationship between their respective mothers. For both, pregnancy partook of mystery. Elizabeth no longer expected to give birth, considering her age; Mary, betrothed but as yet unmarried, hardly expected to reach that stage in her life as a woman so early. Elizabeth's unexpected pregnancy served as a sign from God that Mary's pregnancy was the work of God: "...nothing will be impossible for God" (Lk 1:37). The twins Esau and Jacob, who struggled for power in the womb of Rebekah (Gn 25:22–24), lived out their lives in rivalry. John the Baptist in Elizabeth's womb experienced, as did his mother, the presence of his Messiah and Lord in the advent of the pregnant Mary on her mission of mercy. "And how does this happen to me, that the mother of my Lord should come to me?" (Lk 1:43) Elizabeth recognized Mary as the mother of the Messiah; John the Baptist and his disciples would eventually also recognize the sovereignty of Jesus: "...one mightier than I is coming" (Lk 3:16).

Alternative first readings are offered in the lectionary. The Song of Songs, a series of wedding lyrics traditionally attributed to the much-married Solomon, usually accompanied the feast of the Visitation when it was celebrated on July 2 in the pre-1969 lectionary. The dialogue of lover and beloved is liturgically used to suggest the encounter of Mary and Elizabeth, Jesus and John the Baptist. "My lover speaks; he says to me,/ 'Arise, my beloved, my beautiful one,/ and come!' " (Sg 2:10) The other alternative, excerpted from Zephaniah, occurs in the lectionary as the first reading for the third Sunday of Advent (C). The joy of the prophet and of Jerusalem derived from the closeness of the Lord in the Temple: "Fear not, O Zion, be not discouraged!/ The LORD, your God, is in your midst,/ a mighty savior" (Zep 3:16–17).

That intimate presence of God-with-us ("Immanuel": Is 7:14), whether in the Temple on Mount Zion or in the womb of Mary (Mt 1:23), frames the sentiment of the O-antiphon for this day: "O Emmanuel, God's presence among us, our King, our Judge: come and save us, Lord our God!"

December 22

Readings: 1 Samuel 1:24–28; Luke 1:46–56

Childlessness in a traditional society is regarded as tragedy; too often today, in modernized societies, it seems chic. *Seems* is the right word: the efforts of many childless couples and even unmarried men and women to adopt are often frustrated by the lack of children available for fosterage or adoption, at least in the United States—one of the more depressing results of widespread abortion. The first reading, the responsorial verses and the gospel for this late Advent weekday center on the experience of childless women who eventually find themselves mothers or mothers-to-be. The story of the first woman, Hannah the mother of Samuel, has heavily affected, in literary terms, the story of the second, Mary the mother of Jesus. The midrashic connection between them may explain why, in church tradition, the scripturally unmentioned mother of Mary is called Anna (or Ann), the Latinate form of Hannah.

The narrative of Hannah's long childlessness and the eventual birth of Samuel as an answer to her prayers comes early on in that section of the Hebrew Bible that Jews call "the former Prophets." Samuel ends the era of the judges, of whom he is the greatest, and inaugurates the monarchy (reluctantly) and its divine counterbalance, the independent prophetic office. Just as the continuance of Abraham's descent was challenged by the age of the childless Sarah, the beginning of both the monarchy and prophecy was blocked unless Hannah brought forth Samuel. The first reading recounts how Hannah and her husband Elkanah brought their just-weaned son to Yahweh's temple at Shiloh, dedicating him as a nazirite to serve in the holy place. "I prayed for this child, and the LORD granted my request" (1 Sm 1:27). The responsorial verses are excerpted from the canticle of Hannah that follows this narrative, the imagery of which suggests that Hannah thought of her joy as a military victory: "My heart exults in the LORD,/ my horn is exalted in my God. I have swallowed up my enemies;/ I rejoice in my victory" (1 Sm 2:1).

The gospel passage, the Magnificat or canticle of Mary, could as easily be the canticle of Elizabeth, her pregnant kinswoman, or of both together. Luke or his early church sources, very probably Jewish Christian, modeled Mary's canticle on Hannah's, at least partly. The church sings this song of Mary's every evening in the office of Vespers or Evening Prayer. The political vigor of Mary's canticle, like the military imagery of Hannah's, reminds us that this "handmaid of the Lord" (Lk 1:38) was initiating a new and more perfect monarchy and more perfect prophecy through the child in her womb. "[God] has shown might with his arm,/ dispersed the arrogant of mind and heart./ He has thrown down the rulers from their thrones/ but lifted up the lowly./ The hungry he has filled with good things;/ the rich he has sent away empty" (Lk 1:51–53).

The O-antiphon for this day salutes the monarch born of this queen mother: "O King of all nations, source of your Church's unity and faith, come and save all humanity, your own creation!"

December 23

Readings: Malachi 3:1–4, 23–24; Luke 1:57–66

The priestly office and the prophetic charism are contrasted by the great German sociologist Max Weber; the former assures continuity in religious terms and the latter stirs up renewal in the same context. In Judea, after the Babylonian exile, with the Davidic monarchy abolished, the Levitical priesthood took over more than the ritual life of the Jews, serving as administrators (or even lackeys) for various imperial overlords: Persian, Syrian-Greek, Roman. Prophecy became more and more anonymous, and finally silent, as the centuries passed. One anonymous prophetic voice is ascribed to a critic of the priesthood usually referred to as Malachi, but his name derives from the first words in chapter 3, verse 1: "my messenger." The Book of Malachi is usually placed at the end of the prophetic works in the Old Testament, partially because the gospel writers saw it—in tandem with Isaiah, the first in editorial order—as pointing to the advent of Jesus and John the Baptist, notable critics of the Jerusalem priesthood in their day. "Lo, I am sending my messenger/ to prepare the way before me;/ And suddenly there will come to the temple/ the LORD whom you seek,/ And the messenger of the covenant whom you desire./ Yes, he is coming, says the LORD of hosts" (Mal 3:1).

The birth of John the Baptist, announced in the gospel passage on December 19, takes place in the gospel passage today. The Virgin Mary and John the Baptist are the only figures, other than Jesus, whose birth into this world we celebrate as feasts (September 8 and June 24). For most saints we celebrate the feasts of their births into eternal life (for Mary, August 15 and for John the Baptist, August 29). But the birth of Mary (not narrated in the gospels) and the birth of John the Baptist have a special significance for us who live with the life of her Son, the one whose way John came to make ready (Lk 3:4). Zechariah had not believed the word of the angel about the birth of John, and as a sign he was struck dumb until it occurred. When asked to indicate what the child was to be named on the day of his circumcision, Zechariah agreed with Elizabeth—an agreement he had to indicate by writing—that "John is his name" (Lk 1:63). Such agreement with both God's angel and his wife unlocked Zechariah's tongue, as tomorrow morning's gospel will indicate most eloquently.

Does the name *John* have some extraordinary significance? Ordinarily, Palestinian Jews of the first century A.D. named sons after their grandfathers, and even if Zechariah may have looked old enough to be John's grandfather, it seems odd that their neighbors and relatives were urging the elderly couple to name the child Zechariah. A shorter form of *Jochanan, John* means that "Yahweh has been merciful." Divine mercy breaks the prophetic silence of God for many centuries as well as the physical silence of Zechariah, enabling him to utter on God's behalf something and someone utterly new.

The O-antiphon for this day echoes the canticle of Zechariah (tomorrow morning's gospel): "O Dayspring, splendor of eternal light, sun of justice: come and shine on those lost in the darkness of death!"

December 24 (Morning)

Readings: 2 Samuel 7:1–5, 8–11, 16; Luke 1:67–79

Just as the Magnificat is always the New Testament canticle in the Vespers or Evening Prayer of the church, the Benedictus is always the New Testament canticle in the Lauds or Morning Prayer of the church. Suitably enough, the gospel reading that features the Benedictus, the canticle of Zechariah on the occasion of the naming and circumcision of John the Baptist, is proclaimed only at a morning mass on December 24. An evening mass uses the liturgical readings for the vigil of Christmas and the Evening Prayer has its own Magnificat antiphon, not one of the O-antiphons, and the solemnity of the Lord's Birth has its own three sets of mass readings for midnight, dawn and daytime. The Benedictus is a great prayer for morning—more precisely, for dawn—centered as it is on Jesus as "the Dayspring" who "will visit us/ to shine on those who sit in darkness and death's shadow,/ to guide our feet into the path of peace" (Lk 1:78–79).

The first reading for this morning's mass and the responsorial psalm (89), the same as those used for the fourth Sunday of Advent (B), narrate how God built a household for David rather than have David build a house for God: "Your house and your kingdom shall endure forever before me; your throne shall stand firm forever" (2 Sm 7:16); "I have made a covenant with my chosen one,/ I have sworn to David my servant:/ Forever will I confirm your posterity/ and establish your throne for all generations" (Ps 89:29–30). Such extravagant and unconditional promises to David and his descendants made the Jews after the Babylonian exile, when no descendant of David ruled in Jerusalem, look forward to a day to dawn on which one would.

Zechariah, released from nine months' imprisonment in silence, burst into a canticle that celebrates the advent of this Messiah, the royal heir of David. "Blessed be the Lord, the God of Israel,/ for he has visited and brought redemption to his people./ He has raised up a horn in the house of David his servant" (Lk 1:68–69). The house of David was restored to the throne in Jesus, even if he mounted that throne only on the cross. Only secondarily did the birth of his son John, like Zechariah a member of the priestly tribe of Levi, occupy the father. "And you, child, will be called prophet of the Most High,/ for you will go before the Lord to prepare his ways,/ to give his people a knowledge of salvation/ through the forgiveness of their sins" (Lk 1:76–77). Like the dawn star, John the Baptist willingly faded away with the rising of the sun.

The Solemnity of the Birth of the Lord (CHRISTMAS)

"...a child is born to us...." (Is 9:5)

Mass of the Vigil
December 24
(Afternoon/Evening)

Readings: Isaiah 62:1–5; Acts 13:16–17, 22–25;
Matthew 1:1–25

The prolific American novelist Mary Lee Settle has authored a series of five novels on the theme of freedom, tracing its fortunes through three and a half centuries of the lives of a series of English and American families, somewhat interrelated, starting in the period of the English civil war of the 1640s and ending in West Virginia in 1960, as recollected in 1980. The whole series is called The Beulah Quintet and the pivotal novel that traces the American beginnings of several of the families in eighteenth-century Virginia bears the title *O Beulah Land!* What or who is the Beulah of the titles? In Hebrew *be-ulah* means "married woman" and in the Hebrew scriptures the bearer of that title is the land of Judah itself, rediscovered by the Jewish exiles returning from Babylon. The earlier prophetic tradition had often dwelt on the image of Israel as Yahweh's bride, most notably Hosea, who portrayed Israel as an unfaithful bride. Third Isaiah, the source of this vigil's first reading, assures the desolate Jewish homeland that all her preexilic infidelities are forgiven: "You shall be called by a new name/ pronounced by the mouth of the LORD..../You shall be called 'My Delight,'/ and your land 'Espoused' " (Is 62:2, 4).

The expectation of something better in the future for God's people suffuses this liturgy of the word for the vigil of Christmas. Saint Paul, preaching to the Jewish diaspora community at Antioch in Pisidia, assures them that a new descendant of David has come as the Messiah, the anointed king of Israel. "From [David's] descendants God, according to his promise, has brought to Israel a savior, Jesus" (Acts 13:23). Matthew, whose genealogy of Jesus and account of his birth has been treated above on December 17 and 18, provides the continuous narrative of the genealogy and the birth once again as the gospel for this vigil mass. Hints are given throughout the genealogy of "Jesus Christ, the son of David, the son of Abraham" (Mt 1:1) that this royal descendant of David, one born of a line with many genealogical irregularities in it, will be different. The Epistle to the Ephesians (5:21–33) presents this new David as more than a king, as Yahweh himself, the Bridegroom of the new Israel, the church. As the Book of Revelation comes toward its completion, it looks forward to the consummation of the marriage between the new Jerusalem and the Lamb of God (21:1–9).

December 25
Mass at Midnight

Readings: Isaiah 9:1–6; Titus 2:11–14; Luke 2:1–14

Gifts

Let's face it: all of us as children thought of Christmas as a time for receiving gifts. Advent was the season for finding out where our ingenious parents had hidden them. Boys, at least, were always disappointed to get practical gifts like clothing. The ambiguity we discovered in Christmas gifts ("Nice socks. Thanks, Aunt Jane.") may derive, in some sense, from something mysterious in the very nature of gift giving. Marcel Mauss (1872–1950), Emile Durkheim's nephew and intellectual heir, wrote an engaging monograph precisely on *The Gift,* dealing with the many ways in which traditional societies have understood exchanges of goods other than the purely economic. Pointedly, Mauss underlines "the danger represented by the thing given," noting that the German word *Gift* means "poison" while the English cognate means "a present."

As adults, we might well look for the meaning of Christmas precisely as the celebration of God's bestowal upon humankind of a pure gift. First Isaiah, excerpted in the first reading of the mass at midnight, looks on the birth of King Ahaz's son Hezekiah in the eighth century B.C. as a pure gift from God: "For a child is born to us, a son is given to us;/ upon his shoulder dominion rests./ They name him Wonder-

Counselor, God-Hero,/ Father-Forever, Prince of Peace" (Is 9:5). In the long run, however, Hezekiah disappointed First Isaiah and others who saw him as God's gift to Judah in its moment of peril. No human ruler can ever live up to our hopes for something better, someone better. Jesus, truly divine and truly human, relieves merely human rulers of unrealistic demands by those who would deny them feet of clay.

First Isaiah's hope that the royal birth would give light to "those who dwelt in the land of gloom" (Is 9:1) was fulfilled in what the second reading, an excerpt from the Epistle to Titus, calls "the appearance of the glory of the great God and of our Savior Jesus Christ" (Ti 2:13). The glory of the Lord–an image of Yahweh's presence as refulgent light outweighing and finally overcoming darkness–struck fear into the hearts of ordinary mortals in the Old Testament. According to one strand of biblical tradition, only Moses could speak with Yahweh face to face (Ex 33:11). As a result, his fellow Israelites could not look directly, even at the face of Moses, reflecting as it did the glory of God, forcing Moses to veil his countenance (Ex 34:29–35). Although, in the transfiguration, three disciples caught a glimpse of the nearly blinding glory of God enfleshed in Jesus (Mk 9:2–3), throughout his mortal career Jesus made that glory more accessible to them. Such accessibility of God's glory is "the grace of God" (Ti 2:11) to which the epistle alludes.

In the dark of midnight the glory of the Lord glowed like a conflagration around shepherds near Bethlehem, the birthplace of the shepherd David who became a king (1 Sm 16:11–13). These "shepherds in that region living in the fields and keeping the night watch over their flock" (Lk 2:8) little understood what happened when "the angel of the Lord appeared to them and the glory of the Lord shone around them" (Lk 2:9). The angel of the Lord in any Old- or New-

Testament setting is not an individual, somehow both winged and invisible to the ordinary eye, but something much more profound: a self-presentation of God, mysteriously manifest, delivering a divine word to beings of flesh and blood. The angel of the Lord *is* the glory of the Lord surrounding us, speaking to us.

What word of God did the angelic manifestation of divine glory bring? "Do not be afraid; for behold, I proclaim to you good news of great joy that will be for all the people" (Lk 2:10). When God in the Gospel of Luke brings the message of fearlessness, he usually goes by the name of Gabriel (see Lk 1:13, 30), the demonstration of God's power. The irony of what follows in Gabriel's tidings surrounds the fact that God's power, both Messiah and Lord, came to us clothed in human weakness. "And this will be a sign for you: you will find an infant wrapped in swaddling clothes and lying in a manger" (Lk 2:12). Like every mortal being, the newborn makes his entry onto the human stage in swaddling clothes.

The Alexandrian Jewish Book of Wisdom, composed in Greek in the century just before the birth of Jesus, puts into the mouth of Solomon, the paragon of wisdom, the humble admission that "I too am a mortal man, the same as all the rest..../I too, when born, inhaled the common air,/ and fell upon the kindred earth;/ wailing, I uttered that first sound common to all./ In swaddling clothes and with constant care I was nurtured./ For no king has any different origin or birth,/ but one is the entry into life for all; and in one same way they leave it" (Wis 7:1, 3-6). The sign of the infant wrapped in swaddling clothes, like that of the corpse of the man who was taken down from the cross and wrapped in fine linen and laid in a tomb (Lk 23:53), points to the central mystery of Christian faith: what later theology called the incarnation, the enfleshment of God in history.

The glory of God, manifest normally "in the highest," took on the risk of offering itself as on earth as "peace to those on whom his favor rests" (Lk 2:14). What greater gift—what more generous grace—could Christmas bring?

Mass at Dawn

Readings: Isaiah 62:11–12; Titus 3:4–7; Luke 2:15–20

A New Day

Failed countries are often most easily recognized by the desertion of the streets of their capital cities. With the dissolution of orderly government, economic life ceases and the Hobbesian war of all against all robs these cities of bustling crowds and every other sign of life. The mass at dawn begins with a brief reading from Third Isaiah (a later excerpt from the same chapter with which the vigil mass began) centered on the restoration of deserted Jerusalem after the Babylonian exile. Earlier in the chapter the prophet had spoken of Jerusalem as newly married after a long period of abandonment by its divine Spouse (Is 62:4–5). In the later portion that divine espousal of Jerusalem is spoken of in more prosaic terms of repopulation: "They shall be called the holy people/

the redeemed of the Lord,/ And you [Jerusalem] shall be called 'Frequented,'/ a city that is not forsaken" (Is 62:12).

The second reading, also from the Epistle to Titus, like the second reading of the mass of midnight, centers on that central doctrine of Paul's writings, justification by faith apart from works of the Law. "When the kindness and generous love/ of God our savior appeared,/ not because of any righteous deeds we had done,/ but because of his mercy,/ he saved us" (Ti 3:4–5). At Christmas, and even more so at Epiphany, the liturgical readings stress the "appearance" of God in Christ, the self-revelation of the absolutely transcendent in the fleshly Messiah of the Jews. God's advent as Savior in Jesus of Nazareth delivers us or saves us from the results of our sins, not because of any good deeds we have done, but because of the one saving good deed of God in Christ. In our baptismal death and resurrection we enter into that saving act, the dying and rising of Jesus, accused of Adam's sin of self-divinization but vindicated by God and raised from the dead. "He saved us through the bath of rebirth/ and renewal by the holy Spirit" (Ti 3:5). Our deserted city is repopulated by God's graciousness.

The gospel of the dawn mass continues the gospel of the midnight mass. The shepherds arrived at the manger and found, not a theophany, but a homeless couple and their newborn infant. Somehow it all made sense to them: "When they saw this, they made known the message that had been told them about this child" (Lk 2:17). Dawn is a good time for understanding, for reflection on mysteries like the infant wrapped in swaddling clothes and lying in a manger, mysteries too great for the light of day or the darkness of night. The shepherds and the Virgin Mary understood that a new day was coming. "Mary kept all these things, reflecting on them in her heart" (Lk 2:19). The little-known readings of the mass at dawn invite us to such intimate reflection as well.

Mass during the Day

Readings: Isaiah 52:7–10; Hebrews 1:1–6; John 1:1–18

In the Bosom of God

Hindus of a Vaishnava piety may find their Lord in images of Vishnu as one or another *avatara* (divine descent), and Hindus of a Shaiva religious inclination may find their Lord in images of Shiva bodied forth in one or another female consort or power (*shakti*). Buddhists, less interested in gods, male or female, eventually imaged the Buddha or various *bodhisattvas* (Buddhas-to-be) in elaborate iconography when late Hellenistic influence was felt in the arts of northwestern India. In some parts of Asia this Buddhist artistic urge went so far as to image the ascetic Buddha as a fat and merry elf, cavorting in ivory to bring good luck to those who rubbed him. But Muslims, Christians and Jews all agree that no one has ever seen God.

Of all the scriptural texts associated with the solemnity of Christmas, none goes further in expressing the deepest mystery of this celebration than the last verse from the gospel of Christmas Day. It begins with a negation, a negation common to all the monotheistic traditions of faith that take their origin from the Middle East: "No one has ever seen God" (Jn 1:18). Muslims insist, in the first half of their profession of faith, against all plurality in the divine realm and its underlying materiality, that there is "no god but God." Jews preserve an aniconic faith derived from the blinding nonvision of Moses, as narrated in one version of the Exodus revelation: "I will make all my beauty pass before you, and in your presence I will pronounce my name....But my face you cannot see, for no man sees me and still lives" (Ex 33:19–20). Is Christianity the exception to the Middle Eastern rule? Yes and no.

Second Isaiah, the source of the first reading in this liturgy of the word, insists that the restoration of the Jews to Jerusalem constituted a visible demonstration of God's activity in this world: "Hark! Your watchmen raise a cry,/ together they shout for joy,/ For they see directly, before their eyes,/ the LORD restoring Zion" (Is 52:8). The prophet goes so far as to develop an image of God's power to save as if God wrestles the enemies of Israel to the ground: "The LORD has bared his holy arm/ in the sight of all the nations;/ All the ends of the earth will behold/ the salvation of our God" (Is 52:10). With such vivid images of Yahweh sketched in the words of the Old Testament, it was only prudent that the Jews were forbidden very much production of plastic imagery in a sacred context. But the New Testament releases the floodgates of imagery when it asserts the enfleshment of God in Jesus. The anonymous Epistle to the Hebrews, excerpted in the second reading, declares that this Son of God "is the refulgence of [the Father's] glory,/ the very imprint of his being" (Heb 1:3). The icon and the statue were born, and no amount of iconoclasm or puritanism could suppress them, whether in a Christmas crib or on a baroque altar triptych.

We have never seen God, as it were, in his naked essence, face to face, but we have seen someone much more important for us: God the only Son. Is this a contradiction in terms, all within the length of one verse? How can we say that "no one has ever seen God" and then say that "The only Son, God, who is at the Father's side, has revealed him"? (Jn 1:18). There is a textual problem with the second part of that final verse in the gospel for Christmas Day. Some manuscripts read "only-begotten God," others "the only-begotten Son," and others simply "the only-begotten." In the long run, however, all come down to the same thing. Earlier in the prologue to John's Gospel the evangelist had said that "the Word was God" (Jn 1:1) and "the Word became flesh" with "the glory of an only-begotten coming from the Father" (Jn 1:14).

Jesus, then, fully God and fully one with us, manifests the unseeable Father in our midst. "The only Son, God, who is at the Father's side, has revealed him" (Jn 1:18). The phrase from The New American Bible translation used in the lectionary, "who is at the Father's side," makes Jesus sound a little too much like a press secretary for God or a director of protocol. The image suggested by the Greek original proves more intimate: "...in the bosom of the Father." The picture suggested derives from the banqueting practice in the ancient Middle East. Lazarus, after a life of destitution spent at the door of the uncaring rich man, spends his time in the world to come in the bosom of Abraham, sharing the patriarch's table as an honored guest (Lk 16:23). The Beloved Disciple, witness of the fourth gospel, had the same position at the Last Supper. "One of his disciples, the one whom Jesus loved, was reclining at Jesus' side" (Jn 13:23). The most honored guest at a banquet would recline on a couch facing the host and thus, in a cer-

"...take the child and his mother, flee to Egypt..." (Mt 2:13)

tain sense, be "in his bosom." The next most honored guest would recline at the host's back and have to signal to the Beloved Disciple to find out from him who would betray Jesus (Jn 13:24–25).

Although there may be no real difference in meaning, Lazarus and the Beloved Disciple are described as being merely "in" or "on" the bosoms of their hosts. But the prologue to John's Gospel may hint at something even more intimate in the relationship between Jesus and the Father. "The only Son, God, the one who is *into* the Father's bosom, has *revealed* him." Furthermore, *revealed* is too weak a word for what the gospel reading describes as the work of God the only-begotten. Without any object specified at all, the gospel text declares that God the only-begotten has *exegeted*, drawn out of itself, told the full story. No mere press secretary, God the only-begotten speaks as the plenipotentiary of the Father from within the Father's breast, the deep recesses of the bosom of God, the abyss of the Godhead. No one has ever seen God or ever will or need to. The Word made Flesh has expressed God in full.

At Christmas we prefer less daunting images of Jesus, the infant lying in a manger or asleep on his mother's breast. The one who issued from the heart of God to tell the full story slept on the breast of his mother and dreamt the dreams of human innocence, an innocence unparalleled since Adam's issuance from the hand of God. The full story to be told, to be *exegeted*, by the Word made Flesh was still to come: cross, tomb, glory. At Christmas we worship a God both visible and invisible. "The Word became flesh/ and made his dwelling among us,/ and we saw his glory,/ the glory as of the Father's only Son,/ full of grace and truth" (Jn 1:14).

Sunday in the Octave of Christmas (Feast of the Holy Family)
December 30
When Christmas Falls on Sunday

*Readings: Sirach 3:2–6, 12–14; Colossians 3:12–21;
(A) Matthew 2:13–15, 19–23; (B) Luke 2:22–40;
(C) Luke 2:41–52*

Family Matters

No matter what good may possibly be discerned in what are euphemistically called "alternative family lifestyles," when push comes to shove, having one father and one mother has much to be said for it. The feast of the Holy Family, celebrated annually in the week after Christmas, reminds us of this truism with the same first and second readings every year. The gospel readings, differing by cycle, give us indications from the infancy narratives of Matthew and Luke that Jesus had a far from ordinary upbringing.

There is something slightly trite about the musings of Jesus ben Sirach about family life. "The LORD sets a father in honor over his children;/ a mother's authority he confirms over her sons" (Sir 3:2). Trite, perhaps, but still a good general rule. Perhaps not so valuable in a modern society are the words of the Epistle to the Colossians on the role of women: "Wives, be subordinate to your husbands, as is proper in the Lord" (Col 3:18). If we don't read in church any more the passage a few verses further on urging slaves to "obey your human masters in everything" (Col 3:22), perhaps we should look elsewhere in the epistolary literature of the New Testament for something less dated about the role of women in the family. Much more important for mothers, fathers, children, uncles, aunts and every other relation in a Christian family are the words that precede it: "[Bear] with one another and [forgive] one another, if one has a grievance against another; as the Lord has forgiven you, so must you also do" (Col 3:13).

A Cycle. The gospel for this year's Sunday after Christmas or feast of the Holy Family gives us Matthew's account of how Joseph, at the bidding of an angelic dream, took Mary and Jesus into Egypt as refugees from Herodian persecution. Coptic Christians, about 10 percent today of the population of that country of more than sixty million people, celebrate this event not as "the flight into Egypt" but as "the entry of Our Lord into the land of Egypt," a point of view a little different from that of the refugee family who went through the process. A Coptic doxology for this feast accentuates the positive: "Be glad and rejoice, O Egypt, with your children and all your borders, for the lover of humankind has come to you, he who is before all ages."

Matthew, from a Jewish point of view, sees Jesus as the new Israel sojourning in the house of slavery, which started out as the place of refuge. Like Israel of old, Jesus and his family could look forward to Exodus. Matthew applies to Jesus the prophetic hope of Hosea: "Out of Egypt I called my son" (Mt 2:15, quoting Hos 11:1). Refugees of every sort–from religious and political persecution or from economic distress–have patrons in the Holy Family taking refuge in Egypt.

B Cycle. Christianity was criticized in the first century A.D., and sometimes later as well when it was first introduced into various cultural settings, for disrupting family life. Jesus himself declared that he came, not to bring peace, but the sword (Mt 10:34), so that "from now on a household of five will be divided, three against two and two against three; a father will be divided against his son and a son against his father, a mother against her daughter and a daughter against her mother, a mother-in-law against her daughter-in-law and a daughter-in-law against her mother-in law" (Lk 12:52–53). The tensions within first-century Palestinian Jewish and Greco-Roman families over members who adhered to the way of Jesus smolder just beneath the surface of this saying.

First-century Christians whose faith in Jesus as Messiah and Lord divided them from kith and kin, along with Christians of later centuries whose discipleship caused them tension with their families, could find comfort in the gospel passage from Luke for this day. Mary and Joseph brought the infant Jesus to the Temple in Jerusalem to present him to the Lord, "redeeming" their first-born according to Jewish tradition. A prophet (Simeon) and a prophetess (Anna) approached them in the Temple precincts and the former's words turned from exultation about the Lord's visitation to foreboding about what this child would mean both for Israel and for his mother. "This child is destined for the fall and rise of many in Israel,...(and you yourself a sword will pierce) so that the thoughts of many hearts may be revealed" (Lk 2:34–35). Even the holy family had to live with the threat of crucifying sorrow, of agonizing choices.

C Cycle. The account of the losing and finding of the child Jesus in the Temple gives very bad example to children on the feast of the Holy Family. But it can also provide consolation to those who sometimes find the relationship between

"...I must be in my Father's house...." (Lk 2:49)

parents and children problematic. From whichever side of that relationship they happen to occupy—whether the "children" involved are now mature adults and the parents senior citizens trying still to share their experience with their offspring or the parents are traversing the heights of their middle years and their offspring are caught up in the dense undergrowth of adolescence—not all is sweetness and light in the parent-child relationship.

The Gospel of Luke, much concerned symbolically with the Temple in Jerusalem, shows Jesus claiming his divine right of inheritance of that sacred place as "my Father's house" (Lk 2:49). What seems in the terms of this world to be disobedience toward Joseph and Mary takes on a different meaning in the whole context of the saving death and resurrection of Jesus, with which the infancy narratives of both Matthew and Luke are primarily concerned. For the sake of the children who may be listening, however, Luke tells us that, apart from this notable example of Jesus running away from home, "he went down with them and came to Nazareth, and was obedient to them" (Lk 2:51).

December 26
Feast of Saint Stephen, First Martyr
Second Day within the Octave of Christmas

Readings: Acts 6:8–10; 7:54–59; Matthew 10:17–22

The crown of martyrdom, an ancient phrase in Christian history, may well derive its imagery from the first martyr in the history of the church, Stephen, whose name derives from the Greek word for a crown, *stephanos.* The celebration of the feast of Saint Stephen immediately after the solemnity of Christ's birth may strike the sentimental as macabre but, along with Saint John the Evangelist, usually identified with the Beloved Disciple (December 27), and the Holy Innocents, the children slain at Herod's command in Matthew's infancy narrative (December 28), Stephen bears witness–*martyrion,* in Greek–to the fleshly reality of God in Christ, the saving reality of that body broken for us and that blood poured out for us. Even if the Holy Innocents and John the Baptist died before him, Stephen was the first consciously Christian witness to shed his blood for the revolution in faith that Jesus began.

The first reading for this feast, as excerpted in the lectionary, gives the listener only the beginning and the end of the process that brought Stephen to his death. Chosen as one of the Seven (ahistorically called deacons) who were to supplement the ministry of the Twelve for the sake of the Greek-speaking diaspora Jews in Jerusalem who had adhered to the way of Jesus, Stephen went beyond works of charity into a lively preaching ministry. Like many of the diaspora Jewish Christians, Stephen saw in Jesus' critique of the Temple a key to the universality of the Christian message, its transcendence of its national origins. Between the opening verses of the first reading and the concluding verses, the debate between Stephen and some of the Greek-speaking Jews in Jerusalem is narrated (Acts 6:11–7:53). Basically, Stephen used Old Testament examples to show that true worshipers of Yahweh could come to God in sacrifice and prayer not only at the Temple in Jerusalem, but anywhere in the world. His doctrine bears a strong family resemblance to that of John's Gospel, where Jesus told the Samaritan woman that "the hour is coming when you will worship the Father neither on this mountain nor in Jerusalem" (Jn 4:21). Finally, Stephen died for the same blasphemy (in the eyes of his executioners) for which Jesus did, the assertion of the union of Jesus, the new Temple of God's presence, with God: "I see the heavens opened and the Son of Man standing at the right hand of God" (Acts 7:56).

The gospel reading reminds us that Jesus had warned all of us who would be his disciples that we will be persecuted. But there is hope that we will also have some of the eloquence of Stephen when the hour to bear witness comes: "You will be given at that moment what you are to say. For it will not be you who speak but the Spirit of your Father speaking through you" (Mt 10:19–20).

December 27
Feast of Saint John, Apostle and Evangelist
Third Day within the Octave of Christmas

Readings: 1 John 1:1–4; John 20:2–8

Early church tradition claims that John, the apostle and evangelist (usually thought to be the same person as "the disciple whom Jesus loved" in the Gospel of John and the brother of James, the son of Zebedee in other gospels), died a natural death at a very advanced age. John's natural death occurred despite unsuccessful attempts to give him a martyr's crown, including one attempt to boil him in oil outside the Latin Gate of Rome, a tale told by Tertullian with little historical basis, but which used to have a feast in the Roman calendar on May 6. More worthy of the quintessential witness of the fourth gospel is the legend preserved by Saint Jerome that his preaching, in his last and most feeble years, came down to one simple exhortation: "Little children, love one another." If Stephen became a witness to the death and rising of Jesus with his blood, John witnessed with his gospel, epistles and the Book of Revelation, all traditionally attributed to him.

The first reading is made up of the trumpet blast with which the first and greatest epistle of John begins. For all the theological and spiritual leanings of the writings ascribed to

John, the writer of the epistle insists on the fleshliness of God in Jesus, against all heretical tendencies to reduce Jesus to a principle or a ghost. "What was from the beginning,/ what we have heard,/ what we have seen with our eyes,/ what we looked upon/ and touched with our hands/ concerns the Word of life" (1 Jn 1:1). In his gospel prologue, John rhapsodized about the Word of God's eternal creative command taking flesh in the concreteness of human history. In this Epistle John offers the fleshliness of the Word as a reason why we must reach out in love to our fellow beings of flesh and blood. "What we have seen and heard/ we proclaim now to you,/ so that you too may have fellowship with us" (1 Jn 1:3).

The gospel reading comes from the resurrection narrative in John's Gospel. No gospel is more insistent than John's on the emptiness of the tomb of Jesus and the strange but real corporeality of the risen Lord, possibly because the evangelist was reacting against those in his community who were trying to assimilate Jesus into a phantomlike manifestation of a god or cosmic principle, one who only pretended to suffer and die as human beings must. "The other disciple whom Jesus loved" (Jn 20:2), a very Johannine figure, saw exactly what Simon Peter saw in the tomb: the carefully arranged grave cloths, wrapped now around nothing at all. But, for all his deferential waiting for Peter to precede him into the empty tomb, the Beloved Disciple did more than observe: "He saw and believed" (Jn 20:8). It is not at all unsuitable that we celebrate so close to the solemnity of the Word's enfleshment the memory of the witness to the Word's enfleshed triumph over the grave.

December 28
Feast of the Holy
Innocents, Martyrs
Fourth Day within the Octave of Christmas

Readings: 1 John 1:5–2:2; Matthew 2:13–18

When Pope John Paul II canonized Edith Stein as a martyr, some elements in the Jewish community objected that she had not died as a Christian martyr but as a Jew (albeit converted to Catholicism and living as a Carmelite nun) in the Nazi persecution of the Jews in Europe. The objection was not really accurate. Edith Stein–Sister Benedicta of the Cross, as she was by that time–was one of the convert Jews rounded up in the Netherlands as retribution against the Catholic bishops of that country for forthrightly denouncing Nazi anti-Jewish savagery. In any case, Catholic practice had already for many years revered the seven sons and their mother (2 Mc 7:1–41) martyred for their fidelity to the Law in the Seleucid persecution of the second century B.C. (who used to have a liturgical commemoration on August 1 in the pre-1969 calendar) as well as the Holy Innocents, the Jewish boys slaughtered by order of Herod the Great, according to Matthew's Gospel.

This third feast of witnesses following the solemnity of Christmas commemorates not only "all the boys in Bethlehem and its vicinity two years old and under" (Mt 2:16) but also their prototypes in the Old Testament, the male children of the Israelites whom Pharaoh wanted destroyed (Ex 1:16, 22). No matter how much Saint Augustine may have insisted on the universality of original sin and its baleful power to exclude dead infants from the joyful vision of God, and no matter how much canonization procedures in modern times have scrutinized whether those who have been murdered in various circumstances died as a result of hatred of the faith or not, the Holy Innocents stand there in Matthew's Gospel, lifting their voices against hard and fast laws as well as iron-eyed tyranny in every age and clime. The innocent victims of famine and flood, urban breakdown and mindless warfare, prenatal murder and postnatal abuse die with these innocent children of Bethlehem and its environs. In a world of mass destruction, and at the end of a century of terrifying power to kill and even more terrifying ability to neglect children, the environs of Bethlehem and the reign of Herod the Great have expanded beyond our worst nightmares.

The first reading from the First Epistle of John, continuing from yesterday, contrasts the darkness of a world where innocents are murdered with the light that comes from God: "God is light, and in him there is no darkness" (1 Jn 1:5). Any way in which we "walk in darkness" (1 Jn 1:6) proves that we have not yet surrendered ourselves totally to the light. Jesus, "an Advocate...the righteous one" (1 Jn 2:1), can cleanse us from our darkness and prepare us to live in the light. It is distinctively Catholic to see the possibility of that light-giving work of Jesus extending its influence even beyond the borders of the visible church, to saints whose only baptism was blood or desire for the light of truth.

December 29
Fifth Day within the Octave of Christmas

Readings: 1 John 2:3–11; Luke 2:22–35

Christmas, celebrated just after the winter solstice, may well have been aimed at a Roman Christian community still hankering for the festival of the Unconquered Sun (*Sol Invictus*) marking the first, slight lengthening of the day and shortening of the night after the darkest day of the year. But even before the ritual needs of the Roman Christian community came into view, the scriptures emanating from the first-century Jewish-Christian communities of the Middle East hovered like a moth around Jesus as the Light of the world.

The gospel reading for this day within the octave of Christmas returns to the Lucan story of the presentation of the child Jesus in the Temple. The prophet Simeon, voicing what may well have been an early Jewish-Christian canticle, spoke of the newborn Jesus as "a light for revelation to the Gentiles,/ and glory for your people Israel" (Lk 2:32). To be light to both Jew and Gentile cost Jesus his mortal life and brought sorrow to his mother as well: "You yourself a sword will pierce" (Lk 2:35). The whole of Luke's Gospel and the Acts of the Apostles play this theme out to operatic completion, demonstrating how the mother church of Jerusalem had to suffer as well in giving birth to a much larger reality.

The first reading, continuing the First Epistle of John, urges us to live with the candor of the light of the world. "I do write a new commandment to you, which holds true in him and among you, for the darkness is passing away, and the true light is already shining" (1 Jn 2:8). The dawning of the messianic era welcomed by Simeon brought with it not a division of the world into Israel as conquerer and the Gentiles as conquered subjects, but God's "salvation...prepared in sight of all the peoples" (Lk 2:30–31). Saved by the child redeemed by the sacrifice of "a pair of turtledoves or two young pigeons" (Lk 2:24, quoting Lv 12:8), the offering of the poor, we are to live in a new type of messianic community, binding Jew and Gentile together in love. "Whoever says he is in the light, yet hates his brother, is still in the darkness. Whoever loves his brother remains in the light" (1 Jn 2:9–10).

December 30
Sixth Day within the Octave of Christmas

Readings: *1 John 2:12–17; Luke 2:36–40*

At the beginning and the end of eras of prophecy and king-ship, in the tradition of Israel, stand women named Hannah or Anna, Hebrew or Greek variants of the same name. Hannah, the mother of Samuel, who bridged the eras of the Judges and the Kings, had no child before the birth of Samuel. The son she had begged from the Lord she then returned to the Lord for his service (1 Sm 1:1–28), which included anoint-ing kings and prophetically denouncing them. The octogenar-ian Anna, "a prophetess," precisely remembered as "daughter of Phanuel, of the tribe of Asher" (Lk 2:36), plays an obscure role in the Gospel of Luke, but she seems to stand for the faithful Jewish poor in spirit who frequented the Temple precincts and prayed, like Hannah at Shiloh, while they "were awaiting the redemption of Jerusalem" (Lk 2:38). Her northern Israelite origins (the tribe of Asher), not unlike those of the Ephraimite Hannah, the mother of Samuel, possibly suggest that the northern tribes of Israel, reunited with Judah in the Temple after nine hundred years of separation (1 Kgs 12:1–25), may find their redemption at last.

The first reading, continued from yesterday's, concentrates on the role of Jesus as the role model of human beings faced (as they thought) with the end of history: "Do not love the

"...his mother kept all these things in her heart." (Lk 2:51)

world or the things of the world" (1 Jn 2:15). In view of history's end, why bother struggling for the good things promised for the future? The struggle began with the couple who presented this child in the Temple, who joined Simeon and Anna in looking forward to a glorious consummation for the Holy City. Should we keep it up? "Sensual lust," John informs us, "enticement for the eyes and a pretentious life...is from the world" (1 Jn 2:16). And yet, by God's gracious intervention, we can break through to that future state of beatitude where "whoever does the will of God remains forever" (1 Jn 2:17).

December 31
Seventh Day within the Octave of Christmas

Readings: 1 John 2:18–21; John 1:1–18

December 31, the end of the civil year in recent centuries, did not always have that status. As the Latin root of the month's name indicates, December used to be the tenth of twelve months when the Roman civil year began in March. But the first reading for this final day of the civil year hints at modern times when it begins with a stern warning: "Children, it is the last hour" (1 Jn 2:18). The theologically embattled Johannine community, bedeviled with many heretical "antichrists" who had seceded from its communion, receives an assurance from its apostolic teacher that "every lie is alien to the truth" (1 Jn 2:21). The problems of this Johannine community did not differ very much from those of the church in any age, confronted and sometimes confused by a vaudeville of theological and spiritual tendencies, some wholesome and some just plain odd. Only "the anointing that comes from the holy one" (1 Jn 2:20) assures us that we are in touch with divinely revealed truth.

Repetition is the mother of studies, according to a Jesuit educational tradition, and the church fills out the octave of Christmas by repeating once more (as it does a third time on the second Sunday of the Christmas season in places where Epiphany is celebrated on January 6) the prologue to the Gospel of John as the gospel reading. The Gospel of John opens with something of a rabbinic scriptural meditation or midrashic elaboration on the first words of Genesis about creation: "In the beginning...God said, 'Let there be light,' and there was light" (Gn 1:1, 3). John describes what God said (the Word) as existing anterior to every other reality and as the very means God used to create everything else. First and foremost, however, God's Word was the first thing God said in the Old Testament: "Let there be light." John equates that Word of God with the light that "shines in the darkness, and the darkness has not overcome it" (Jn 1:5).

The only light of which such a claim can be made is the glory of God. In describing the event of Christmas, John's Gospel insists that the Word not only took flesh but "made his dwelling among us" (Jn 1:14). More literally translated, the Word pitched his tent in our midst. Like Yahweh in the Exodus, accompanying his people in a movable tent-shrine,

God in Christ shared the temporary nature of the accommodations we could give him: flesh and blood. But in that flesh and blood, born of Mary, the glory of the Lord has tented with us forever.

January 1
Octave of Christmas
Solemnity of Mary,
Mother of God

*Readings: Numbers 6:22–27; Galatians 4:4–7;
Luke 2:16–21*

Living with Mystery

There is something a little too serene in most images of the Virgin Mother of God. Artists look at Mary backwards, from this side of the resurrection of her Son and his enthronement with the Father. We see Mary at prayer with the apostles, the holy women, the relatives of Jesus (Acts 1:14). But there is no reason to think that the annunciation occurred while Mary was praying. A modern Yoruba carving from Nigeria depicts Mary engaged in the most mundane of daily duties, pounding tubers in a mortar, when the angel interrupts the human routine. Mystery swoops down on her and on us like that, just when we had other things to do.

On this first day of the civil year, the octave of Christmas, we celebrate with the Virgin Mary her mothering of the child Jesus. Luke's account of the earthly origins of Jesus, more important theologically than historically, provides us with something of a cameo presentation of his entire life, death and resurrection. John the Baptist precedes him in annunciation and birth just as he preceded him in preaching and death. Jesus advances towards the Jerusalem Temple, where he disappears and is rediscovered after three days. A bit like the dumb show in *Hamlet,* the infancy narrative of Luke acts out the plot of the whole gospel in symbolic terms, making more explicit in the process the divine origin of Jesus and the significance for Jew and Gentile alike of his redeeming work.

Three times in Luke's infancy narrative the gospel writer imagines for us Mary's inner thoughts, her contemplative wonder at what she was experiencing. The only adult figure to appear in both the prelude and the main movement of the gospel, Mary is portrayed as a woman struggling with the meaning of what was happening to her and to her child. At the annunciation by the angel Gabriel, "she was greatly troubled at what was said and pondered what sort of greeting this might be" (Lk 1:29). Greater clarity came with the birth of Jesus and the coming of the shepherds, as today's gospel suggests. "Mary kept all these things, reflecting on them in her heart" (Lk 2:19). A more literal translation makes more of Mary's contemplative powers: "Mary held on to all these realities, comparing them with each other." At the conclusion of Luke's infancy narrative, with the story of the loss of the child

Jesus and his recovery in the Temple, Luke returns to the theme of Mary's contemplation: "His mother kept all these things in her heart" (Lk 2:51).

Mary spent her lifetime trying to put together the extraordinary experiences she had with this child, living out the prophetic words of her kinswoman, Elizabeth: "Blessed are you who believed that what was spoken to you by the Lord would be fulfilled" (Lk 1:45). In Luke's account of the public life of Jesus we catch a glimpse of Mary and other relatives of Jesus having a hard time understanding what he was doing with his life. Informed that they were trying to penetrate a crowd that surrounded him, Jesus asked aloud *who* were his mother and his relatives, a question he then answered himself. "My mother and my brothers are those who hear the word of God and act on it" (Lk 8:21). Words calculated to offend? Perhaps not. The infancy narrative suggests that Mary, alone among the relatives of Jesus, deserved a reputation for blessedness, not because of her physical maternity, but because she was one of those "who hear the word of God and observe it" (Lk 11:28).

Saint Paul's only reference to Mary, albeit anonymous, singles out the quintessence of her greatness in the second reading for this solemnity: "When the fullness of time had come, God sent his Son, born of a woman, born under the law, to ransom those under the law, so that we might receive adoption" (Gal 4:4-5). The circumcision of Jesus, also commemorated on this day, entered him into the covenant God made with Abraham (Gn 17:10), confirming his Jewish identity as did his birth from a Jewish mother. The Virgin's willingness to mother this Son in mystery made possible our adoption in mystery into the family of God. Thus adopted, we can call God what Jesus called him in Aramaic, a term almost as intimate as *Papa*. "As proof that you are children, God sent the spirit of his Son into our hearts, crying out, 'Abba, Father!'" (Gal 4:6). The naming of God as Father corresponds on this day with the naming of God's Son, the Virgin's Son, as Jesus, "the name given him by the angel before he was conceived" (Lk 2:21).

Naming God, who transcends all our attempts to pin him down, daunted the Jews, who preserved a commandment given at Sinai that "you shall not take the name of the LORD, your God, in vain" (Ex 20:7). Most Bible translations and the lectionaries adapted from them follow the Jewish tradition of saying "Lord" *(Adonai)* whenever the sacred name "Yahweh" appears in the literal Hebrew text. One day of the year the high priest (Aaron, in the Book of Numbers) was to bless the people with the ordinarily unpronounced divine name: "The LORD bless you and keep you!/ The LORD let his face shine upon you, and be gracious to you!/ The LORD look upon you kindly and give you peace!" (Nm 6:24–26) The first reading for this day enshrines this high priestly blessing, suitable for the first day of the civil year and the octave of Christmas, when the unutterable name of God became the very utterable Jesus.

Through the contemplative willingness of the Virgin Mary to let God's Word take flesh in her womb, we need no longer avoid pronouncing the name of God. Adopted as God's sisters and brothers, we can even call him Jesus.

Second Sunday after Christmas

When Epiphany Is Celebrated on January 6

Readings: Sirach 24:1–4, 8–12; Ephesians 1:3–6, 15–18; John 1:1–18

What God Said

If you did not catch the prologue to John's Gospel in the mass of Christmas Day or the weekday mass of December 31 (the seventh day within the octave of Christmas), you have one more chance outside the United States and other countries where Epiphany is usually celebrated on the second Sunday after Christmas. I myself have only had one occasion to hear this liturgy of the word, but it was memorable, on a cold Sunday morning in the Sinai peninsula, at the foot of Jabal Musa, as the Arabs call it, the mountain of Moses, within view of the Greek Orthodox monastery of Saint Catherine at Mount Sinai. In what more stark environment could one hear the incredible good news that the Word was made flesh and pitched his tent among us?

Both the Old Testament and the New Testament readings for this Sunday look toward the gospel and try to prepare us for it. The first reading for this Sunday, excerpted from the Wisdom of Jesus ben Sirach, concentrates on the fascinating figure of Wisdom (*Hokhmah* in Hebrew, *Sophia* in Greek), conceived of as something of a female emanation from God even before the events of creation and the Exodus. The author finds the lady Wisdom enthroned on the pillar of cloud that guided the people of Israel by day in the Exodus. She also inhabits the tent where Yahweh lived among his people: "He who formed me chose the spot for my tent..../In the holy tent I ministered before him,/ and in Zion I fixed my abode" (Sir 24:8, 10). The first chapter of the Epistle to the Ephesians starts with an exultant prayer of thanksgiving. The author, probably a disciple of Paul in the generation immediately after Paul's death, continues the apostle's vigorous proclamation of the divine predestination of all humanity to be a holy people in Christ, the new Israel: "[God] chose us in him, before the foundation of the world, to be holy and without blemish before him" (Eph. 1:4).

Such imagery of the preexistent will and work of God in the late Old Testament and in the Pauline literature of the New Testament prepares us to hear John's prologue and its presentation of the preexistent majesty of the Word who became flesh to bring us back into union with God. But nothing can really prepare us for the prologue to John. Perhaps that is why the liturgy for many centuries mandated reading it as a thanksgiving at the conclusion of the mass, the so-called "last gospel." We can only come to understand it by repetition, by contemplative osmosis. Meditating like a kabbalist on texts from the account of creation in the first chapter of Genesis, the author of the fourth gospel takes the divine command "Let there be light" (Gn 1:3) as the first and preeminent Word of God, what God said from all eternity. The author then follows the progression of this spoken light into our darkness. A deliberately clumsy translation of the prologue brings out its relationship to Genesis, although it underemphasizes the personhood of the Word. But it may jar us into attending to what the gospel really says.

In the beginning was
WHAT-GOD-SAID.

WHAT-GOD-SAID
was with God.
WHAT-GOD-SAID
was God.
WHAT-GOD-SAID
was with God
in the beginning.
Through WHAT-GOD-SAID
all things came to be.
Not one thing came to be
except through WHAT-GOD-SAID.
All that came to be had life
in WHAT-GOD-SAID
and that life was "LET THERE BE LIGHT"
for humanity,
"LET THERE BE LIGHT" that shines in darkness,
"LET THERE BE LIGHT" that darkness could not overcome.

After a brief allusion to the testimony of John the Baptist to the Word/Light (Jn 1:6–8), the fourth evangelist returns to the central theme.

WHAT-GOD-SAID was really
"LET THERE BE LIGHT"
that enlightens the whole of humanity.
WHAT-GOD-SAID was in the world
that had its being through WHAT-GOD-SAID.

Yet the world did not know WHAT-GOD-SAID.
WHAT-GOD-SAID came to his own people,
but they did not accept WHAT-GOD-SAID.
But to those who did accept WHAT-GOD-SAID,
WHAT-GOD-SAID gave power to become God's children.

These children are those who put their faith
in the Name ("I AM WHO I AM")
of WHAT-GOD-SAID.
They were born not from a blood relationship,
—not from fleshly desire, not from man's desire—
but from God.

WHAT-GOD-SAID
became flesh
and pitched a tent in our midst.
We caught a glimpse of the divine glory
of WHAT-GOD-SAID,
the divine glory that WHAT-GOD-SAID
has from the Father
as the Only Begotten,
filled with the free gift of true fidelity.

The theme of John's witness to the Word/Light returns (Jn 1:15) but the evangelist pays more attention to the enfleshed Word.

From the fullness of WHAT-GOD-SAID
we have all received,
free gift upon free gift.
For the Torah was given through Moses,
but the free gift of true fidelity
came through Jesus, the Messiah.

No one has ever seen God.
God the Only Begotten
–reclining on God's heart–
has made God known.

Indeed, that is the last gospel.

Weekdays between January 1 and Epiphany

Whether Epiphany is celebrated on the Sunday after January 1 (as it usually is in the United States) or on a holiday (January 6), the following sets of readings are prescribed for as many weekdays as intervene, six being the maximum in the United States when January 1 is a Sunday, none when January 1 is a Saturday (Epiphany occurring the next day) and four the maximum when Epiphany is celebrated on a holiday (January 6). The readings for these days are attached to the date in the calendar, but the proper prayers and antiphons go with the day of the week (Monday before Epiphany, etc.).

January 2

Readings: 1 John 2:22–28; John 1:19–28

False messiahs, pretenders to Davidic royal power in the tradition of Israel, much preoccupied the contemporaries of Jesus and other believers, Jewish and Christian as well as Muslim, in later ages. The most famous of these false messiahs in the Jewish tradition, Shabbetai Zevi, a Jew born in Smyrna (Izmir) and raised in the Muslim Ottoman Empire at its zenith, had, with the prompting of the kabbalist Nathan of Gaza, proclaimed the year 1666 as the advent of the messianic era, with himself as the Messiah. Imprisoned in Gallipoli by the Ottoman Sultan (whom he had proposed to dethrone), Shabbetai Zevi became a focus of worldwide Jewish pilgrimage. Threatened by the Ottoman Sultan and his court with execution for the uproar he was causing, Shabbetai Zevi renounced Judaism and became a Muslim, renamed Aziz Mehmet Effendi. Some of his devotees, egged on by Nathan of Gaza, maintained that Zevi had only appeared to apostasize, in the hopes of converting Muslims to his messianic cause. Strange religious cults do not all begin in California.

The false messiahs denounced by Jesus in Matthew's Gospel (Mt 24:24) may well have been both Jewish and Christian, pseudoprophets of the cataclysmic end of the world. In the First Epistle of John, a slightly different term–*antichrist* or *anti-Messiah*–may well designate teachers opposed to the central teaching of the school of the Beloved Disciple, "that Jesus is the Christ" (1 Jn 2:22). What were these teachers proposing? We are not absolutely sure, but it seemed to involve denying "the Father and the Son" (1 Jn 2:22), denying that Jesus was in any realistic sense God's unique Child. The first reading for this second day of the civil year returns to the great theme of the Christmas season: that Jesus, God's Son, has come as the Messiah or Anointed One. Furthermore, our baptismal anointing or christening into him makes us sharers in that divine and human messianic identity: "His anointing teaches you about everything and is true and not false; just as it taught you, remain in him" (1 Jn 2:27). The exhortation of the epistle's author to "remain in him" echoes the famous words on the lips of Jesus in John's Gospel: "Remain in me, as I remain in you" (Jn 15:4).

The gospel reading continues from where the gospel for December 31 leaves off, immediately after the full organ prelude of the prologue to the Gospel of John. John the Baptist in the fourth gospel depicts himself in negatives: not the Messiah, not Elijah and not the prophet-like-Moses spoken of in Deuteronomy 18:18. Despite his nonidentity with these biblical figures thought to initiate a new era with a baptismal regeneration, John did insist on the importance of his own baptismal practice as a foretaste of what will happen when that one comes, "whose sandal strap I am not worthy to untie" (Jn 1:27). The liturgical readings for these days leading up to Epiphany help us to realize why the Baptism of the Lord is not only the second epiphany in the Latin rite but the central Christmas mystery in much of the Christian East.

January 3

Readings: 1 John 2:29 –3:6; John 1:29–34

The Dalai Lama, spiritual head of the Tibetan Buddhist community at home and in exile, is traditionally thought to be a *bodhisattva,* a future Buddha or Enlightened One, who postpones his ultimate enlightenment to rule the Buddhist community of Tibet. At his death, however, an official delegation of lamas searches throughout Tibet for a young child who bears the characteristics that mark him as the new Dalai Lama, and that child is raised to assume the position. In recent years, under Communist Chinese domination, the future of this unusual method of succession has been challenged severely, with the Dalai Lama living in exile in India and the Chinese waiting for his demise in order to subvert the tradition.

The First Epistle of John suggests in today's first reading a somewhat similar concept, that one can recognize the true children of God by their spiritual resemblance to the unique

Child of God, Jesus. "We are God's children now; what we shall be has not yet been revealed. We do know that when it is revealed we shall be like him, for we shall see him as he is" (1 Jn 3:2). The crucifixion of Jesus resulted from the fact that all too many of his contemporaries, those characterized as "the world" because of their attachment to merely mortal values, "did not know [the Son]," and we can hardly expect any better for ourselves from such people. This is why "the world does not know us" (1 Jn 3:1). But if we bear the characteristics of the Son, we shall keep free of sin: "...in him there is no sin" (1 Jn 3:5). Just as the lamas can recognize the characteristics of the next Dalai Lama in little children, we too can recognize the characteristics of God's Son in any person "who remains in him" (1 Jn 3:6).

John the Baptist, in the gospel reading, freely admits that at first he "did not know" (Jn 1:33) Jesus as the one "who ranks ahead of me because he existed before me" (Jn 1:30), perhaps because Jesus was so different from John. But, like the Tibetan Buddhists, John the Baptist eventually recognized the marks of the true Messiah or Anointed One after Jesus had been baptized, an event that John's Gospel does not actually describe: "I saw the Spirit come down like a dove from the sky and remain on him" (Jn 1:32). Very different from the fiercely ascetical Baptist, Jesus is symbolically identified as "the Lamb of God, who takes away the sin of the world" (Jn 1:29). The more we are conformed to Jesus as God's sacrificial Lamb, the more we will be recognized as bearing the characteristics of God's children.

January 4

Readings: 1 John 3:7–10; John 1:35–42

Most Americans fifty years of age or older remember where they were when they first heard the news of President John Fitzgerald Kennedy's assassination on November 22, 1963. An older generation has similar memories of the day President Franklin Delano Roosevelt died, April 12, 1945. Remembering such events in connection with a precise time and place plays an important part in the human imagination. The gospel reading for this weekday before Epiphany records such a piquant detail remembered by the two disciples whom John the Baptist had directed into the followership of the Lamb of God, one of them Andrew and the other presumably the Beloved Disciple who presents the fourth gospel.

When Jesus asked them what they were seeking in following him, they clumsily asked him, "Rabbi..., where are you staying?" (Jn 1:38). He invited them to find out: "Come, and you will see." The gospel writer notes parenthetically that "they went and saw where he was staying, and they stayed with him that day. It was about four in the afternoon" (Jn 1:39). What these two disciples experienced that late afternoon made it memorable for them. They hardly knew what they were looking for when they undertook to follow the Lamb of God, and the fact that Andrew announced to his brother Simon Peter that "We have found the Messiah" (Jn 1:41) indicates that their understanding of the Lamb of God may have been far from complete after that first encounter.

But a revolution in their religious sensibilities had begun, and many decades later the gospel witness dated it to a particular late afternoon.

The First Epistle of John also looks for a revolution in religious sensibilities in the followers of Jesus. "No one who is begotten by God commits sin, because God's seed remains in him; he cannot sin because he is begotten by God" (1 Jn 3:9). We have all fallen into sin, despite our baptismal grafting onto God's stock, but time is still left to us, despite the lateness in the afternoon, to stay with Jesus for the rest of the day.

January 5

Readings: 1 John 3:11–21; John 1:43–51

Christians are called *Nasara* in the Qur'an–"Nazarenes," because they are identified in the original Arab Muslim imagination with the people of the town of Nazareth in Galilee, where Jesus was raised. According to Luke's Gospel the preaching of Jesus, although welcomed at first with interest in Nazareth (4:22), eventually encountered murderous hostility in the town of his upbringing (4:28–30). The gospel for today narrates how Jesus called Philip to be his disciple and Philip in turn called Nathanael. Elsewhere in John's Gospel we learn that Nathanael hailed "from Cana in Galilee" (Jn 21:2), not exactly a great metropolis, but his humble origins did not keep Nathanael from expressing incredulity that "the one about whom Moses wrote in the law" (Jn 1:45) could have had his roots in such an insignificant town: "Can anything good come from Nazareth?" (Jn 1:46).

Jesus took no offense at the slighting of Nazareth and seems to have engaged Nathanael in a little obscure but delightful banter. "Here is a true Israelite. There is no duplicity in him" (Jn 1:47). The quotation is ambiguous; it could be either pure praise (translated as it stands) or something more ironic: "Here's someone genuinely Israelite, in whom there is no guile." The term *Israelite* in the Greek of the New Testament may possibly mask the Hebrew and Aramaic term *child of Israel,* in which case it could suggest a relationship between Nathanael and Jacob/Israel of the Genesis narrative, a man known for his guile (Gn 25:27–34; 27:1–40; 30:25–32:3). Thus the sentence may read: "Here's someone genuinely Israel's descendant, but without the guile." Not at all embarrassed by what he perceived as high praise, Nathanael asked Jesus how he knew of his virtue. No one is quite sure what Jesus meant by his reply: "Before Philip called you I saw you under the fig tree" (Jn 1:48). So impressed was Nathanael by this foresight that he bestowed on Jesus messianic titles: "You are the Son of God; you are the King of Israel" (Jn 1:49). Jesus assured Nathanael and the readers of the fourth gospel that they were yet to learn that Jesus is much more than the king of Israel, that he is, in fact, the place where God's messengers descend to earth and ascend to heaven, as in Jacob/Israel's dream at Bethel (Gn 28:10–19).

"God is greater than our hearts and knows everything" (1 Jn 3:20), as the first reading assures us. He knows what we did or didn't do under the fig tree, good or bad. The first Epistle of John urges on its readers and hearers the priority of love in the moral life. "We know that we have passed from death to life because we love our brothers" (1 Jn 3:14). If we live out the sacrificial love of Jesus in our own lives, laying down our lives in service, we will know what the life and love of Jesus were all about: "The way we came to know love was that he laid down his life for us; so we ought to lay down our lives for our brothers" (1 Jn 3:16).

January 6

Readings: 1 John 5:5–13; Mark 1:7–11

In the tradition of the Latin rite of the Catholic Church there are three epiphanies or manifestations of the Lord. The antiphon before the canticle of Zechariah (the Benedictus) in Morning Prayer for the solemnity of Epiphany spells this liturgical tradition out: "Today the Bridegroom claims his bride, the Church, since Christ has washed her sins away in Jordan's waters; the Magi hasten with their gifts to the royal wedding; and the wedding guests rejoice, for Christ has changed water into wine, alleluia." In that particular antiphon the Baptism of the Lord is presented as the central panel of a triptych, a tradition even more intelligible in those churches of the Middle

East that make much more of the baptism of Jesus in the Jordan as the central Christmas mystery than they do of his birth at Bethlehem. What I grew up calling "Little Christmas"– the Epiphany–is not so little at all for the Coptic Christians of Egypt, who normally celebrate the mystery on January 7 (the equivalent of December 25 in the Julian calendar). Normally, however, despite the above-quoted antiphon, the Latin rite makes the manifestation of Jesus as newborn King of the Jews to the Gentile Magi the central panel of its Epiphany triptych.

Having exhausted the first chapter of John's Gospel over the weekdays since December 31, the church directs our attention today to the most basic account of the baptismal epiphany of Jesus, that narrated by Mark. Matthew's account of the same event takes an apologetic stance for the fact that Jesus was baptized for sin, featuring John the Baptist demurring and Jesus insisting on the ritual abasement (Mt 3:14–15). Luke's Gospel tucks the baptism away into a subordinate clause (Lk 3:21), emphasizing in the main clause the manifestation of the Spirit and the divine designation of Jesus as God's beloved Son (Lk 3:22). John's Gospel, as mentioned earlier, never really describes the baptism of Jesus, alluding only to the descent of the Spirit (Jn 1:32–33).

But Mark takes the baptism of Jesus on directly. Before the passage excerpted in today's gospel, Mark narrates how "People of the whole Judean countryside and all the inhabitants of Jerusalem were going out to him and were being baptized by him in the Jordan River as they acknowledged their sins" (Mk 1:5). In today's gospel excerpt Mark laconically mentions that "it happened in those days that Jesus came from Nazareth of Galilee and was baptized in the Jordan by John" (Mk 1:9). No excuses are offered for the association of Jesus with sinners, but a hint is given almost immediately that God vindicated him from all the charges laid against him, and most notably the sin of Adam and Eve, attempting to "be like gods who know what is good and what is bad" (Gn 3:5; see also Jn 10:33). The vindication arrives with dramatic suddenness: "On coming up out of the water he saw the heavens being torn open and the Spirit, like a dove, descending upon him. And a voice came from the heavens, 'You are my beloved Son; with you I am well pleased'" (Mk. 1:10–11).

The First Epistle of John makes reference to three witnesses to the real identity of Jesus as the unique Son of God: "...there are three that testify, the Spirit, the water, and the blood, and the three are of one accord" (1 Jn 5:7–8). This trinity of witnesses seems to evoke not only the blood and water that flowed from the side of the dead Jesus in John's account of the passion (Jn 19:34), concrete reminders of his physicality against all who would reduce him to a phantom, but also the Spirit that he handed over with his dying breath (Jn 19:30). But the mention of the Spirit as a witness also echoes what John the Baptist had said of the descent of the Spirit on Jesus: "John testified further, saying: 'I saw the Spirit come down like a dove from the sky and remain upon him. I did not know him, but the one who sent me to baptize with water told me, "On whomever you see the Spirit come down and remain, he is the one who will baptize with the holy Spirit" ' " (Jn 1:32–33). The Spirit that descended on Jesus after his baptism in the waters of the Jordan is handed over in turn to us when he sheds his blood on the cross. If Jesus is in a theological sense the one sacrament of God, the effective outward sign of God's salvific will, it is possible to see in this text from the First Epistle of John the gradual articulation of that sacrament into baptism with water and the Spirit, feeding us with Christ's body and blood and the confirmation and ordination by the power of the Spirit. The sacraments manifest God in Christ through the power of the Spirit, and this sacramental manifestation of the divine is what we mean by *epiphany*.

January 7

Readings: 1 John 5:14–21; John 2:1–12

The third epiphany in the tradition of the Latin rite surrounds what Jesus, in John's narrative, did at Cana in Galilee, the "beginning of his signs" (Jn 2:11). This gospel passage designated for today also occurs on the second Sunday in Ordinary Time in Cycle C, one week after the solemnity of the Baptism of the Lord, providing a link between the Advent-Christmas-Epiphany cycle and Ordinary Time in that year. Only seven miraculous signs occupy the central stage in the first half of John's Gospel, and each is carefully narrated and replete with symbolic meaning. Each Johannine sign is, as it were, an epiphany, a manifestation of God's saving presence in very concrete settings.

The wedding feast to which the mother of Jesus, Jesus himself and his disciples had been invited should not be treated as an ordinary event, with the wine running out because bibulous disciples put a strain on the supply. The wedding of Yahweh with Israel or Jerusalem plays a symbolic role in the

"Woman, how does your concern affect me?" (Jn 2:4)

prophecies of Hosea (2:21–23), Ezekiel (16:8–14), Second Isaiah (54:4–8) and Third Isaiah (62:4–5), with the human partners often unfaithful despite God's fidelity. The eschatological era features a great deal of wine imagery in the work of several of the prophets, most notably Amos (9:13) and Joel (4:18). In the context of this wedding in John's Gospel, the mother of Jesus (never called Mary in the fourth gospel) implicitly asks her son for something he is reluctant to give, precisely because to give this sign of divine power–to accede to the epiphany–threatens him with the hour of his personal *eschaton*, a source of dread for Jesus in John's Gospel (Jn 12:23–28). "The mother of Jesus said to him, 'They have no wine.' [And] Jesus said to her, 'Woman, how does your concern affect me? My hour has not yet come' " (Jn 2:3–4). This first mention of the hour of Jesus complements its mention in the context of another banquet, the Passover seder on the night before his death: "Before the feast of Passover, Jesus knew that his hour had come to pass from this world to the Father" (Jn 13:1).

The mother of Jesus did not take these words of Jesus as a refusal to come to his hour. In this first of two glimpses of her in the fourth gospel, her faith motivates her to direct the waiters at the feast to "do whatever he tells you" (Jn 2:5). What Jesus did in response involved much more than the provision of eschatologically abundant wine. He commanded the waiters to fill with water six enormous stone jars, the type "for Jewish ceremonial washings" (Jn 2:6). The transformation of the means of legal purity into the stuff of hilarious superfluity may strike the sober-sided reader with horror, to say nothing of those who laid such great emphasis on the law of legal purity (Mk 7:1–8). Abstemious apostles of temperance in modern times have tried, rather comically, to suggest that the outcome of the miraculous sign that Jesus worked was the production of some curious concoction called "nonalcoholic wine." The wine provided by Jesus far exceeded the quantity of wine provided by the host, and far excelled its quality as well, not unlike the wine he told his disciples he would drink "with you new in the kingdom of my Father" (Mt 26:29).

The first reading for this day, taken from the First Epistle of John, assures us that we can expect the Lord to hear our prayers: "We have this confidence in him, that if we ask anything according to his will, he hears us" (1 Jn 5:14). Every prayer that prefaces its specific requests with the general proviso that "your will be done,/ on earth as in heaven" (Mt 6:10) receives at least that answer: God's will is done. This may not be very satisfying for us in emotional terms, but it helps to keep us realistic in our dealing with God. Among the more serious requests we should make from God is that life will be given to the sinner (cf. 1 Jn 5:16). Jesus eventually came to the cross precisely to fulfill such prayer, to make it possible for us to be "in the one who is true, in his Son Jesus Christ. He is the true God and eternal life" (1 Jn 5:20).

Solemnity of the Epiphany
Second Sunday after Christmas where January 6 is not a holiday

Readings: Isaiah 60:1–6; Ephesians 3:2–3, 5–6; Matthew 2:1–12

Homage

In A.D. 66, Tiridates, Parthian ruler of Armenia, traveled overland to Italy to present himself to the Emperor Nero. Mazdean religious taboos prevented Tiridates from traveling more efficiently by sea. Political considerations–and especially the desire to flatter Nero into granting virtual autonomy to the fiefdom of Armenia–suggested to the crafty Parthian astrologers who accompanied Tiridates on the journey that they should proclaim that they had seen in the stars Nero's ascent to the universal rule of the west. They also counseled Tiridates to return to Armenia by a different route, once again involving as little transportation over water as possible. The memory of this royal progress from the east to the west and back may well have left an impression on the mixed Jewish-Gentile Christian community for whom Matthew wrote his gospel. The story of the Gentile Magi paying homage to the infant Jesus enabled Matthew to engage the attention of the members of that mixed community in the birth of the Jewish Messiah, helping the Gentile members to join their fellow

"Where is the newborn King of the Jews?" (Mt 2:2)

Christians who were Jews in asking the question, "Where is the newborn king of the Jews?" (Mt 2:2).

What did Matthew mean by *Magi*? The original Magi, a priestly caste or tribe of the Medes flourishing in the sixth century B.C., survived the absorption of Media into the burgeoning Persian Empire. They may have been responsible, much later, for diverting the monotheistic Zoroastrians into twinning Ahura Mazdah (the Wise Lord) with Angra Mainya (the Evil One) as creations of impersonal Zurvan (Time). In the first century of the Christian era, their name was given to all sorts of magicians, charlatans and practitioners of quackery in the Roman Empire, from which the Emperor Tiberius banished them in A.D. 19. The Gospel of Matthew treats them more generously, even though Magi come in for bad notices from Luke in the Acts of the Apostles, where one (Simon Magus) introduced simony into the history of the church (Acts 8:9–24) and the other provoked Paul to strike him blind (Acts 13: 6–12).

A bit like New Age gurus in contemporary Europe and America, the Magi of the gospel era claimed to be practicing occult "sciences," and such claims fascinated those who found themselves disenchanted with the passé Greek and Roman pantheons and the faded clarities of Stoic philosophy. Greek-speaking Gentiles, and some assimilated Jews as well, looked to the East for religious stimulation. Matthew, living in such a situation of religious restlessness, presents the Messiah of the Jews as the true object of this Gentile search for meaning. Had Matthew written in our day, the Magi might have been maharishis.

The Latin rite of the Catholic Church celebrates the manifestation of the newborn King of the Jews to the Gentile Magi or astrologers as the central panel in its triptych of epiphanies. Third Isaiah, from which the first reading for this solemnity derives, celebrates the restoration of Jerusalem and the

Temple after the Babylonian exile and looks forward to a time when Jerusalem will welcome righteous Gentiles who seek to bask in the light of God's dwelling place on earth. "Nations shall walk by your light,/ and kings by your shining radiance" (Is 60:3). The last verse excerpted in the first reading numbers among future pilgrims to Jerusalem three of Abraham's descendants by his third wife, Keturah (Gn 25:1–4): "Caravans of camels shall fill you,/ dromedaries from Midian and Ephah;/ All from Sheba shall come/ bearing gold and frankincense,/ and proclaiming the praises of the LORD" (Is 60:6). The following verse from Third Isaiah, not included in the lectionary excerpt, mentions also two of the descendants of Hagar, Abraham's exiled Egyptian wife (Gn 25:12–16), along with Midian, Ephah and Sheba, easily identified as ancestors of the Arabs: "All the flocks of Kedar shall be gathered for you,/ the rams of Nebaioth shall be your sacrifices;/ They will be acceptable offerings on my altar,/ and I will enhance the splendor of my house" (Is 60:7). The hope of Third Isaiah for the reunion of the Israelites and the Gentiles of the Arab world around the Temple in Jerusalem still eludes us many centuries later. In the mystery of the manifestation of the newborn King of the Jews to Gentiles, however, the child of promise (Isaac) and the child driven with his mother into the desert (Ishmael) can find reconciliation at last.

Picking up the theme of reconciliation of the Chosen and the non-Chosen in the messianic future, the Epistle to the Ephesians, from which the second reading derives, follows the Pauline tradition by addressing the Gentile Christians of Ephesus as brothers and sisters in faith, one with faithful Jews. "The mystery...was not made known to human beings in other generations as it has now been revealed to his holy apostles and prophets by the Spirit, that the Gentiles are coheirs, members of the same body, and copartners in the promise in Christ Jesus through the gospel" (Eph 3:3,5–6). It is not surprising, given the themes of these Epiphany readings, that Pope John Paul II has chosen this solemnity, year after year, to ordain bishops to serve in dioceses in many parts of the Catholic world, old and new, on every continent. Epiphany reminds us that *Catholic* means "universal."

The gospel narrates not only the quest of the Magi but also the quandary it posed for Herod the Great. An Idumean by tribal background who was, in some sense, half-Jewish, Herod ruled both Idumea (ancient Edom) and Judea for the Romans for more than thirty years. Idumeans in general and Herod in particular suffered from an identity crisis. Forcibly converted to Judaism in the reign of John Hyrcanus (134–104 B.C.), the Idumeans mixed their religious observances in a way most offensive to devout Jews. Although Herod began the reconstruction of the Jerusalem Temple on a magnificent scale, he also refurbished the shrines of his Idumean ancestors' gods. Knowing how hated he was by the Jews, Herod plotted to instigate general mourning at the time of his own death by mandating the simultaneous execution of leading Jews in the hippodrome of Jericho. Happily, his funeral plans were aborted.

"[Herod] was greatly troubled" (Mt 2:3) at the news that the visiting astrologers had seen among the signs of the zodiac a star indicative of the fact that a new king had been born to rule the Jews. Unfamiliar with many of the details of Jewish messianic expectation, Herod ascertained from "the chief priests and the scribes of the people" (Mt 2:4) that a true descendant of David was expected to be born in Bethlehem, where David had been born. Like so many other devious tyrants, Herod befriended the Magi and asked them to "search diligently for the child...[and] bring me word, that I too may go and do him homage" (Mt 2:8). Fortunately for the newborn King of the Jews, the Magi, after presenting their gifts of gold, frankincense and myrrh (the first two borrowed from Isaiah 60:6), "having been warned in a dream not to return to Herod, ...departed for their country by another way" (Mt 2:12). Did the itinerary of Tiridates affect Matthew's telling of this tale?

Presenting the mystery of the entry of God in Christ into our history, the evangelist Matthew situates the conjunction of God with humanity in the last years of Herod's tyranny. Like Moses in Egypt, Jesus in Idumean-dominated Palestine posed a threat to despotism. The mythic Magi, seekers of truth from the Gentile world, reminded not only the half-Jewish Herod of his identity problem, but also Matthew's half-Jewish, half-Gentile community of theirs. Matthew, like Saint Paul, saw his community's mixture of Jewish and Gentile identity not as a problem but as an opportunity, a signal of the manifestation of God in the flesh for all of humanity. To be both Jewish and Gentile, the child of a Jewish mother and a Gentile father, is both a problem and an opportunity. Like every form of mixed parentage, such dual identity points towards the miscegenation of God and humankind that we call incarnation.

Monday after Epiphany

Readings: 1 John 3:22–4:6; Matthew 4:12–17, 23–25

Galilee at the time of Jesus presented peculiar challenges and considerable problems for a faithful Jew. After the Assyrian invasion of Galilee in the 730s B.C., the Assyrian ruler Tiglath Pileser III deported the local populations, dispersing them throughout his expanding empire. Thus came to birth the so-called lost tribes of Israel. Galilee's reputation for Yahwistic faith suffered because of this deportation of its Israelite natives and the subsequent settlement there of diverse Gentile populations. Even in the first century A.D. Galilee retained its name (coined by the eighth-century-B.C. Isaiah) as "Galilee of the Gentiles" (Is 8:23 as cited in Mt 4:15). Not unsuitably for the Epiphany season, the gospel for this day portrays Jesus bringing the Good News to this semi-Jewish, semi-Gentile borderland. Matthew assures us that this preaching was heard even beyond Jewish territories: "His fame spread to all of Syria….great crowds from Galilee, the Decapolis, Jerusalem, and Judea, and from beyond the Jordan followed him" (Mt 4:24–25).

The First Epistle of John sums up the Good News in two commandments: "We should believe in the name of his Son, Jesus Christ, and love one another just as he commanded us" (1 Jn 3:23). How does this differ from the double commandment Jesus enunciated in the Gospel of Mark? "The first is this: 'Hear, O Israel! The Lord our God is Lord alone! You shall love the Lord your God with all your heart, with all your soul, with all your mind, and with all your strength.' The second is this: 'You shall love your neighbor as yourself'" (Mk 12: 29–32, citing Dt 6:4–5 and Lv 19:18). At first blush there seems to be a radical difference in the first commandment or the first half of the commandment, but this proves not to be true on further examination of what the Johannine writer means by the phrase, "believe in the name of his Son, Jesus Christ."

The name of Jesus, in this setting, is not *Jesus* but what Saint Paul called "the name that is above every other name" (Phil 2:9), the almost unutterable divine name of *Yahweh*. Ascribing that name to Jesus, proclaiming that Jesus the Messiah is Lord (see Phil 2:11), lies at the foundation of Christian faith. The monotheistic faith of Jews is not compromised in the Johannine writing of the New Testament but focused on the Word made Flesh, whose oneness with the Father and oneness with us provide the basis for the union of keeping faith with God and loving our neighbor. Thus "every spirit that acknowledges Jesus Christ come in the flesh" (1 Jn 4:2) fulfills both commandments. At the center of the mystery of Epiphany stands the union of flesh and spirit, humankind and the Lord, love of neighbor and love of God.

Tuesday after Epiphany

Readings: 1 John 4:7–10; Mark 6:34–44

The Irish writer James Joyce used the term *epiphany* to designate certain moments in his fiction in which a character recognizes in a startling and concrete fashion something not previously realized. In his short story, "The Dead," the last in the collection entitled *Dubliners*, the epiphany experienced by the main character, Gabriel Conroy, takes place after a Twelfth Night (Epiphany eve) musical soirée. Conroy is deeply in love with his wife and also prone to somewhat bombastic rhetoric about the virtues of those long dead in his family and circle of friends who began this tradition of Epiphany musicales. He finds at the conclusion of the night that his wife's distracted air when a tenor sings the mournful song, "The Lass of Aughrim," stems from the fact that it had been sung for her many years before by a long dead adolescent sweetheart of whom her husband knew nothing. The much lauded dead of the past come back to haunt him.

Mark and Matthew (twice) and Luke and John (once) each narrate an epiphany experience that Jesus made possible many times for his disciples and the large crowds who came to hear his words. Initiating an act of commensality by bidding his disciples to feed a multitude of five thousand in a deserted place, Jesus made possible a glimpse of God's bountiful care for his people by multiplying "five loaves and the two fish" (Mk 6:41) with such generosity that "they picked up twelve wicker baskets full of fragments and what was left of the fish" (Mk 6:43). The concentration on the bread and the comparative neglect of the fish in each gospel account of this epiphany of God's power in a concrete setting suggests that the evangelists saw in it a foretaste of the eucharistic "breaking of the bread" (Acts 2:42) that was to play such a central role in the Christian memorialization of the saving Passover of Jesus. "Then, taking the five loaves and the two fish and looking up to heaven, he said the blessing, broke the loaves, and gave them to [his] disciples to set before the people; he also divided the two fish among them all. They all ate and were satisfied" (Mk 6:41–42).

Mark tells us that when "[Jesus] saw the vast crowd, his heart was moved with pity for them, for they were like sheep without a shepherd; and he began to teach them many things" (Mk 6:34). That pity of Jesus, the motivation for the epiphany of God's power that he effected in multiplying the bread and fish, demonstrates quite clearly what the First Epistle of John, excerpted in the first reading, means when it says that "God is love" (1 Jn 4:8). Divine power demonstrated apart from divine love can only terrify sheep without a shepherd. The Good Shepherd of the Johannine tradition of the New Testament does much more than drive the sheep: "A good shepherd lays down his life for the sheep" (Jn 10:11). The First Epistle of John states this in less imagistic terms: "In this is love: not that we have loved God, but that he loved us and sent his Son as expiation for our sins" (1 Jn 4:10). It is not hard to see why Luke narrates that the Good News of the birth of Jesus was first announced to shepherds.

Wednesday after Epiphany

Readings: 1 John 4:11–18; Mark 6:45–52

Mark, Matthew and John all connect with the feeding of the five thousand a subsequent epiphany of God in Jesus' coming to the disciples in a storm on the Sea of Galilee. The conjunction of miraculous feeding with the conquest of water suggests the signs of God's power made manifest in the Exodus of the Israelites from Egypt. Mark's account makes less of the fierceness of the storm than do Matthew and John, but it does note that Jesus saw their plight from the vantage point he had when he "went off to the mountain to pray" (Mk 6:46). Mark alone of the three evangelists who narrate this story states that Jesus "alone on shore" saw the disciples in their boat "tossed about while rowing, for the wind was against them" (Mk 6:47–48). Between three and six in the morning, as dawn was breaking, "he came towards them walking on the sea. He meant to pass by them" (Mk 6:48), a majestic movement suggestive of Yahweh's passing before Moses (Ex 33: 18–19). The description suggests further that "they thought it was a ghost and cried out. They had all seen him and were terrified" (Mk 6:49–50). Was the original context of this epiphany a resurrection appearance of Jesus? Why else would the disciples fear Jesus as a ghost?

Jesus demonstrated that he was not only not a ghost but that he was more than a miracle-working mortal prophet. Using the divine name to identify himself, "At once he spoke with them: 'Take courage, it is I, do not be afraid' " (Mk 6:50).

"It is I" is, in Greek, more literally, "I am," the core of the divine name revealed to Moses in the burning bush (Ex 3:14). The command "Do not be afraid" is a typical "holy war" motif in the earliest passages of the Old Testament (e.g., Ex 14:13; 20:20; Dt 1:29; Jos 1:9, etc.), a command backed up by the assurance that Yahweh is with his people in their struggle against incredible odds. Jesus overcame the disciples' fear by sharing their plight, being with them as Yahweh was with the Israelites in the Exodus, now not as a pillar of fire and cloud but as a fellow passenger in the beleaguered boat: "He got into the boat with them and the wind died down" (Mk 6:51). Mark, as usual, notes that the disciples missed the point of this epiphany as they missed the point of the multiplication of the loaves: "They were [completely] astounded. They had not understood the incident of the loaves. On the contrary, their hearts were hardened" (Mk. 6:51–52).

Because God "has given us of his Spirit" (1 Jn 4:13) and "God remains in us" (1 Jn 4:12) as the source of the love we have for one another, we can overcome the obtuseness of Mark's disciples. "No one has ever seen God" (1 Jn 4:12), the author of the First Epistle of John insists, as does the fourth gospel: "No one has ever seen God. The only Son, God, who is at the Father's side, has revealed him" (Jn 1:18). We can continue that epiphany of God's love for us enfleshed in Jesus and poured out in the Spirit. "God is love, and whoever remains in love remains in God and God in him" (1 Jn 4:16). To continue that epiphany of God's love we have to overcome the fear of love: "One who fears is not yet perfect in love" (1 Jn 4:18). Jesus, who loved his friends and his enemies, showed us the way and, even more importantly, enabled us to love as he did: "Whoever acknowledges that Jesus is the Son of God, God remains in him and he in God" (1 Jn 4:15).

Thursday after Epiphany

Readings: 1 John 4:19–5:4; Luke 4:14–22

"Home is the place where, when you have to go there,/ they have to take you in," wrote Robert Frost in his famous poem of 1914, "The Death of the Hired Man." The ambiguities of home, its potent combination of the intimate and comforting as well as the intimidating and oppressive, lie behind these pregnant lines of verse. Jesus, like every prophet, had mixed feelings about Nazareth, his hometown. The gospel reading for this weekday of Epiphany ends before the evangelist tells us how the hometown crowd in Nazareth rose up against Jesus and tried to kill him (Lk 4:28–30).

But things started off better. After Jesus quoted a combination of two texts from Third Isaiah (Is 61:1–2 and Is 58:6), proclamations that Yahweh had appointed Third Isaiah "to bring glad tidings to the poor./ He has sent me to proclaim liberty to captives/ and recovery of sight to the blind,/ to let the oppressed go free,/ and to proclaim a year acceptable to the Lord" (Lk 4:18–19), Jesus told his fellow Nazarenes that "Today this scripture passage is fulfilled in your hearing" (Lk 4:21). The people of Nazareth eventually rejected the epiphany of the Lord's prophetic spirit in Jesus, but at first they were better disposed, perhaps for the wrong reasons: "All spoke highly of him and were amazed at the gracious words that came from his mouth" (Lk 4:22). The words that immediately follow in Luke, not included by the lectionary editors, hint at the rejection that was coming: "They also asked, 'Isn't this the son of Joseph?' " (Lk 4:22).

Like the people of Nazareth, we all find it difficult to hear God's word spoken to us by close relatives and friends: Familiarity breeds contempt. The First Epistle of John brings the love of God down to concrete instances when it insists that "whoever does not love a brother whom he has seen cannot love God whom he has not seen" (1 Jn 4:20). Not only does Jesus, the only-begotten, reveal God (Jn. 1:18); everyone begotten of God gives us a chance to glimpse the only-begotten. "Everyone who believes that Jesus is the Christ is begotten by God, and everyone who loves the father loves [also] the one begotten by him" (1 Jn 5:1). Jesus, thought to be the son of Joseph, a mere carpenter, commanded little respect in Nazareth. In this Epiphany season we need to examine ourselves, questioning our willingness to realize the many epiphanies of God and Christ in our neighbors and friends and even, sometimes, those we may be tempted to define as our enemies.

Friday after Epiphany

Readings: *1 John 5:5–13; Luke 5:12–16*

NOTE: The first readings for the Friday and Saturday of the week after Epiphany are the same as the first readings for January 6 and 7 when Epiphany is celebrated on the second Sunday after Christmas occurring as late as January 7 or 8, although the gospels for these days differ. Thus the reflections on these first readings for January 6 and 7 are reprinted below. These readings would never occur on both January 6 and 7 and the Friday and Saturday after Epiphany in the same liturgical year. When Epiphany, celebrated on the second Sunday after Christmas, occurs as late as January 7 or 8, the week after Epiphany is suppressed and the feast of the Baptism of the Lord follows on the Monday following the second Sunday after Christmas.

The first Epistle of John makes reference to three witnesses to the real identity of Jesus as the unique Son of God: "There are three that testify, the Spirit, the water, and the blood, and the three are of one accord" (1 Jn 5:7–8). This trinity of witnesses seems to evoke not only the blood and water that flowed from the side of the dead Jesus in John's account of the passion (Jn 19:34), concrete reminders of his physicality against all who would reduce him to a phantom, but also the Spirit that he handed over with his dying breath (Jn 19:30). But the mention of the Spirit as a witness also echoes what John the Baptist had said of the descent of the Spirit on Jesus: "John testified further, saying, 'I saw the Spirit come down like a dove from the sky and remain upon him. I did not know him, but the one who sent me to baptize with water told me, "On whomever you see the Spirit come down and remain, he is the one who will baptize with the holy Spirit"'" (Jn 1:32–33). The Spirit that descended on Jesus after his baptism in the waters of the Jordan is handed over in turn to us when he sheds his blood on the cross. If Jesus is in a theological sense the one sacrament of God, the effective outward sign of God's salvific will, it is possible to see in this text from the First Epistle of John the gradual articulation of that sacrament into baptism with water and the Spirit, feeding with Christ's body and blood and the confirmation and ordination by the power of the Spirit. The sacraments manifest God in Christ through the power of the Spirit, and this sacramental manifestation of the divine is what we mean by *epiphany*.

The gospel reading dramatically illustrates Jesus as an epiphany of God's power to heal and save. A leper–someone assiduously avoided in ancient times, when every skin disease was classified as leprosy until proven otherwise (Lv 13:1–14:57)–kept his distance from Jesus when he begged him for a miraculous cleansing. "When he saw Jesus, he fell prostrate, pleaded with him, and said 'Lord, if you wish, you can make me clean' " (Lk 5:12). Jesus could have cured the man at a hygienic distance, but he chose not to: "Jesus stretched out his hand, touched him, and said, 'I do will it. Be made clean' " (Lk 5:13). The word *touch* is a bit too weak in this translation; the Greek of Luke suggests that Jesus stretched out his arm and grasped the leper. In the parallel passage in Mark (1:40–45) the evangelist remarks that, when the matter of this healing of a leper became known, "it was impossible for Jesus to enter a town openly. He remained outside in deserted places, and people kept coming to him from everywhere" (Mk 1:45). Part of this derives, no doubt, from the

Marcan theme of Jesus avoiding the revelation of his "messianic secret." Is there a hint as well that Jesus was in some sense polluted by the embrace of a leper as far as his contemporaries were concerned? The epiphany of God in Christ does not shrink away from the pain of the human condition.

Saturday after Epiphany

Readings: 1 John 5:14–21; John 3: 22–30

On the eve of the feast of the Baptism of the Lord, when it occurs on the third Sunday after Christmas, the church directs our attention once more to John the Baptist, the dominant figure of mid-Advent. John's Gospel never gives a description of the baptism of Jesus, although John the Baptist testified that he "saw the Spirit come down like a dove from the sky and remain upon him" (Jn 1:32). Later in the gospel, in the passage excerpted for the liturgy of the word today, we are given a glimpse of a certain rivalry between the movement surrounding Jesus and that surrounding John. "Jesus and his disciples went into the region of Judea, where he spent some time with them baptizing. John was also baptizing in Aenon near Salim, because there was an abundance of water there, and people came to be baptized" (Jn 3:22–23). A little later in

John's Gospel the author seems to contradict the impression here given that Jesus himself baptized others: "although Jesus himself was not baptizing, just his disciples" (Jn 4:2).

A Judean with whom John had engaged in controversy about ritual purification, who may have suggested that Jesus and John differed on this subject, had apparently raised the topic with disciples of the Baptist. In any case, the disciples of John the Baptist felt some chagrin over the growth of the movement surrounding Jesus and they seemed to want to provoke their master to jealousy of Jesus: "Rabbi, the one who was with you across the Jordan, to whom you testified, here he is baptizing and everyone is coming to him" (Jn 3:26). With disciples like that who needs opponents? John, true to his declaration that "I am not the Messiah...I was sent before him" (Jn 3:28), resorted to a homely image of his status in comparison with that of Jesus: "The one who has the bride is the bridegroom; the best man, who stands and listens for him, rejoices greatly at the bridegroom's voice" (Jn 3:29). A model of selflessness, the Baptist pointed not to himself but to the Light.

The first reading for this day, taken from the First Epistle of John, assures us that we can expect the Lord to hear our prayers: "We have this confidence in [God] that if we ask anything according to his will, he hears us" (1 Jn 5:14). Every prayer that prefaces its specific requests with the general proviso that "your will be done,/ on earth as in heaven" (Mt 6:10) receives at least that answer: God's will is done. This may not be very satisfying for us in emotional terms, but it helps to keep us realistic in our dealing with God. Among the more serious requests we should make from God is that life will be given to the sinner (cf. 1 Jn 5:16). Jesus eventually came to the cross precisely to fulfill such prayer, to make it possible for us to be "in the one who is true. And we are in the one who is

true, in his Son Jesus Christ. He is the true God and eternal life"
(1 Jn 5:20).

Feast of the Baptism
of the Lord

*Readings: Isaiah 42:1–4, 6–7; Acts 10:34–38;
(A) Matthew 3:13–17; (B) Mark 1:7–11;
(C) Luke 3:15–16, 21–22.*

Christmas in certain churches of the East occurs in early
January and dwells thematically less on the birth of Jesus at
Bethlehem than on his baptism by John in the Jordan. A folk
custom beloved of the Greek Orthodox, even in the cold of
January in New York, involves young Greek swimmers retriev-
ing a cross cast into the sea as a symbol of Christ's descent
into the depths at his baptism and his rising from the waters
to new life, marked out as God's Son by the epiphany of the
Spirit. Every baptism in the Christian tradition enacts a symbolic dying and rising, a ritual drowning and rebirth. Each of
the synoptic gospels narrates a version of the baptism of
Jesus, while John's Gospel only mentions the descent of the
Spirit (Jn 1:32). The three liturgical cycles in the lectionary

"I need to be baptized by you...." (Mt 3:14)

each has its own gospel account of the baptism of Jesus, but the first and second readings of this feast are the same in every cycle.

The first song of the Servant of Yahweh, excerpted from Second Isaiah, possibly referred in its original setting to the role of Israel after the Babylonian exile. No longer trying to model itself on Solomon as a potent source of power in the Middle East, Israel, in the vision of Second Isaiah, is merely God's servant, albeit a servant much beloved by his divine Master: "Here is my servant whom I uphold,/ my chosen one with whom I am pleased,/ Upon whom I have put my spirit" (Is 42:1). Among the attributes of this new and humble Israel are enumerated gentleness ("Not crying out, not shouting,/ not making his voice heard in the street": Is 42:2) and perseverance in the task of carrying out Yahweh's will ("he shall bring forth justice to the nations": Is 42:1). The suggestion that Israel can serve the Gentiles ("the nations") as a model of justice or righteousness indicates that Second Isaiah thought of Israel as having something of a missionary task. This first Servant Song in Second Isaiah clearly affected all three gospel accounts of the baptism of Jesus, and especially this first Servant Song's notice that God has endowed the servant with his Spirit. Even before the Servant Songs affected the gospel writers they seem to have inspired Jesus himself to take on the form of a Servant and to shun the trappings of a messiah.

The second reading, an excerpt from the Acts of the Apostles, gives us an example of the preaching of the earliest Christian generations. Luke here records words attributed to Peter addressing the Gentile household of Cornelius, an Italian soldier in the occupying Roman force in Palestine. In the late first century A.D., with the destruction of the Temple and the excommunication of Jewish Christians from the more general Jewish community as heretics, the followers of the Way of

Jesus became predominantly Gentile. The household of Cornelius–Gentile proselytes of the Jewish tradition contemporary with Peter–provided a model for what the church was eventually going to be, not a sect of Judaism but a new religious movement, developing considerably the universalistic style of Judaism foreshadowed in Old Testament writings like Jonah, Ruth and Second Isaiah.

Peter, having been told by God in a visionary experience that no animal is unclean in God's eyes (Acts 10:13–15), discovered as well that not only animals but Gentiles have been made clean by divine decree: "I see that God shows no partiality. Rather, in every nation whoever fears him and acts uprightly is acceptable to him" (Acts 10:34–35). The source of that cleansing, according to Peter, was "the word [that] he sent...as he proclaimed peace through Jesus Christ, who is Lord of all" (Acts 10:36). The proclamation of that good news dated from the time when Jesus of Nazareth, "beginning in Galilee after the baptism that John preached" was anointed by God "with the holy Spirit and power" (Acts 10:37–38). If the first reading, from Second Isaiah's first Song of the Servant of Yahweh, suggested the identification of Jesus with Yahweh's gentle Servant, the sermon of Peter in Acts emphasizes that in that servanthood Jesus both experienced and communicated the powerful influx of God's Spirit. In his baptism, sinless for the sins of others, Jesus underwent symbolically a death and resurrection, a death and resurrection as a vicarious suffering Servant who would by his sufferings justify many (see Is 52:13–53:12).

Cycle A. Matthew's account of the baptism of Jesus makes much of the role of John the Baptist in the event. Whereas Mark presents the baptism of Jesus among repentant sinners without any embarrassment, Matthew has John the Baptist protest: "I need to be baptized by you, and yet you are coming to me!" (Mt 3:14). The reply of Jesus to this protest hints at an entire theology of redemption by vicarious suffering: "Allow it now, for thus it is fitting for us to fulfill all righteousness" (Mt 3:15). John and Jesus realized that in this baptism for sins they were participating in a larger mystery. John was called to collaborate with Jesus in making possible righteousness–justification in the sight of God–for all humankind. By his baptism as a commitment to die for sins, Jesus consecrated or sacrificed himself (Jn 17:19), or, in another way of expressing it, "God anointed Jesus of Nazareth with the holy Spirit and power" and "he went about doing good and healing all those oppressed by the devil, for God was with him" (Acts 10:38).

Cycle B. Mark's account of the baptism of Jesus, less concerned with the fact that Jesus was baptized among sinners (Mk 1:5), stresses instead the descent of the Spirit on the newly baptized Jesus. The excerpt from the Gospel of Mark used for this feast begins with the mention of the fact that John the Baptist had declared: "I have baptized you with water; he will baptize you with the holy Spirit" (Mk 1:8). Mark seems to imply that Jesus himself first experienced his radical relationship to God in the immediate aftermath of his baptism amid sinners. That experience came to Jesus in the form of a voice from heaven and the descent of a dove: "On coming up out of the water he saw the heavens being torn open and the Spirit, like a dove, descending upon him. And a voice came from the heavens, 'You are my beloved Son; with you I am well pleased'" (Mk 1:10–11). The voice from heaven hints at a symbolic link between the newly baptized Jesus and Isaac about to be sacrificed by Abraham: "Then God said: 'Take your son Isaac, your only one, whom you love, and go to the land of Moriah'" (Gn 22:2). The detail mentioned by Mark that Jesus saw "the sky rent in two" may hint at a relationship to the psalmlike passage in Third Isaiah where the prophet expresses the wish that God "would rend the heavens and come down" (Is 63:19). The power of the Most High overshadowing Mary (Lk 1:35) and the Spirit descending on Jesus in the form of a dove were one and the same God breaking into our universe, leaving the remoteness of the heavens and willing to dwell among us.

Cycle C. Luke's account of the baptism of Jesus tells us that John the Baptist looked forward to Jesus baptizing "with the holy Spirit and fire" (Lk 3:16). In the Advent season we heard also of John's expectation that the Messiah who would come would have "his winnowing fan...in his hand to clear his threshing floor and to gather the wheat into his barn, but the chaff he will burn with unquenchable fire" (Lk 3:17). In contrast with these fierce expectations of John the Baptist, Jesus experienced his relationship to God less austerely: "After all the people had been baptized and Jesus also had been baptized and was praying, heaven was opened and the holy Spirit descended upon him in bodily form like a dove. And a voice came from heaven, 'You are my beloved Son; with you I am well pleased' " (Lk. 3:21–22). Luke almost tucks away the baptism by John, so intent is he on emphasizing the intimate relationship between Jesus and God's Spirit, a relationship experienced in prayer.

The dove that descended on Jesus in all four gospels bears a strong resemblance to the image of Israel itself, the dove of the psalms (e.g., Pss. 74:19; 68:14) and the beloved of Yahweh in one interpretation of the Song of Songs: "O my dove in the clefts of the rock,/ in the recesses of the cliff,/ Let me see you" (Song 2:14). The prophet Jonah, whose name means 'dove' in Hebrew, had to deal with the hated Ninevites (Jn 3:1–4:11) as the Servant of Yahweh had to deal with Jew and Gentile alike, "Not crying out, not shouting,/ not making his voice heard in the street" (Is 42: 2). In some sense, with the descent of the Spirit of God on Jesus in his baptism, Jesus became a new Israel, a new Jonah sent to bring good news to Gentiles as well as Jews. The interlocking seasons of Advent, Christmas and Epiphany come to a fitting conclusion with this image of Jesus arising from the depths of his baptism and receiving the Spirit he will hand on to all humankind, Jew and Gentile alike.

The
Saints
of
Advent,
Christmas
and
Epiphany

During this season the church urges us to make every effort to use the readings assigned to particular days in the Advent-Christmas-Epiphany cycle. Only one feast (Saint Andrew, November 30) and one solemnity (Immaculate Conception, December 8) have readings that preclude use in the liturgy of the word of the lectionary pericopes for those weekdays, apart from the saints celebrated as part of the octave of Christmas on December 26, 27 and 28. Memorials of other saints can be made in the presidential prayers of the liturgy. There follows a few brief reflections on each of these saints memorialized in the general liturgical calendar as well as those whose memorials are particularly kept in the United States.

November 30
Feast of Saint Andrew, Apostle

Readings: Romans 10:9–18; Matthew 4:18–22

Saint Andrew not only introduced his brother Simon Peter to Jesus, according to John's Gospel (Jn 1:40–41), but he also introduces the Advent season to the church, which has defined Advent as beginning on the Sunday on or nearest Saint Andrew's feast day in such a way that four Sundays occur before the solemnity of Christmas. As a result, Saint Andrew's feast day is sometimes celebrated shortly before Advent begins, or else early in the first week of Advent. Even in Advent the readings for his feast take precedence over those of an Advent weekday.

The Greek (and other Byzantine, especially Russian) churches and the Scottish churches look to Andrew in a special way as their patron, the former because ecclesiastical traditions assert that Andrew preached the gospel in Greece and died there, martyred on an X-form cross. (The cross of Saint Andrew, white on a blue field, serves as the flag of Scotland; combined with the cross of Saint George, it is known as the Union Jack, the flag of the United Kingdom.) Andrew's name in Greek, *Andreas* ("virile"), indicates that he was known by his Gentile name rather than the Hebrew one, perhaps because, along with his brother Simon Peter, he grew up in the Roman vacation resort of Bethsaida (Jn 1:44). Evidently he not only bore a Greek name but spoke Greek and could, with his fellow townsman Philip, interpret for those Greek-speaking pilgrims who had traveled to Jerusalem to seek an interview with Jesus (Jn 12:20–22).

The first reading for Saint Andrew's feast, excerpted from Paul's Epistle to the Romans, reflects Andrew's vocation as an apostle, a church-founder who brought the Good News to Gentiles, and especially to the Greeks. "There is no distinction between Jew and Greek; the same Lord is Lord of all, enriching all who call upon him" (Rom 10:12). Paul spells out the essence of the apostolic or missionary vocation as a commitment to preach the word of revelation to be accepted by its hearers in faith: "How shall they call upon [the Lord] in whom they have not believed? And how can they believe unless they have heard of him? And how can they hear unless there is someone to preach? And how can men preach unless they are sent?" (Rom 10:14–15). The gospel reading, Matthew's account of the call of the disciples to be "fishers of men" (Mt 4:19), portrays "Simon who is called Peter, and his brother Andrew" (Mt 4:18) as the first to be called, the first to be invited, first to hear and then to preach. "At once they left their nets and followed him" (Mt 4:20). We could do no better than that in the season of Advent.

December 3
Saint Francis Xavier,
Priest and Missionary

On December 3, 1552, Francisco de Yasu y Javier—to give the Spanish form of his name—died of a fever on the island of Sancian, off the coast of China, at the age of forty-six. For a little more than ten years before that Xavier had worked indefatigably in the evangelization of parts of India, Indonesia and Japan; in the last-named he was the first Christian missionary. Hoping to spread the Good News to China as well, he headed in that direction but died before reaching the coast. One of the original companions of Ignatius Loyola, founder of the Society of Jesus (Jesuits), Xavier shares with Saint Thérèse of Lisieux (d. 1897) the title of patron saint of the missionary outreach of the church. His popularity as a patron saint is attested by various versions of his name given to men at baptism, especially in Latin countries, where there are many Javiers and Saverios, and in the English-speaking world, where one can always guess the religious background of someone whose first initials are F. X., including at least one famous woman, Saint Frances Xavier Cabrini (d. 1917; feast: November 13). Xavier once wrote to Ignatius Loyola that, when he saw the enormous work needed to spread the Good News in Asia, he wished that he could return to the place of his university studies in Paris and, "crying out like a madman, riveting the attention of those with more learning than charity," beg his fellow scholars to attend to the crying spiritual needs of the new Christians, actual and potential, of the East.

December 4
Saint John Damascene,
Priest and Teacher

A Syrian of Greek cultural patrimony born around A.D. 645 in the early years of Muslim Arab rule over Syria, John of Damascus (Yahya al-Mansur in Arabic) followed his father in the profession of civil servant of the Umayyad dynasty (661–750). John eventually resigned his position around the year 700, frustrated by systematic prejudice against Christians under the caliph ʿAbd al-Malik (r. 685–705). Becoming a monk at the monastery (still functioning) of Mar Saba in Palestine, John turned his considerable literary talents to the service of the church, taking on the Iconoclasts, heretics determined to wipe out the artistic traditions of the Byzantine churches. Precisely because he lived in former Byzantine territory now ruled by the Muslim Arabs, John did not suffer the wrath of Iconoclastic Byzantine officialdom, although it condemned his writings after his death. This took place when John was more than one hundred years of age, thereby proving that austere monastic life and theological controversy are better for your health than a civil service position. The seventh General Council (Nicaea II) in 787 vindicated John's orthodoxy, and he is esteemed, to the present day, as the last of the Greek fathers of the church.

December 6
Saint Nicholas, Bishop

Saint Nicholas, Bishop of Myra in what is now Turkey but more revered at Bari in Italy, probably lived in the fourth century A.D. He has given his name and most of his reputation to Santa Claus. Virtually every story told of him is legendary, including his feats as a dowry provider for orphan girls otherwise condemned to prostitution. His generous gift of three bags of gold as a dowry has made him the patron saint of pawn brokers, who have transformed the bags into three golden balls. Nicholas probably survived the 1969 purge of legendary figures in the calendar of the saints because the Germans, the Swiss and the Dutch use his feast day as a time for giving gifts to good children and (at least in principle) coal to bad children. Like Saint John of Damascus and Saint Andrew, Nicholas is much revered in both the Byzantine and Latin branches of Christendom. The Muslim conquest of Eastern Christendom eventually prompted the transfer (not to say theft), in the eleventh century, of the relics of Saint Nicholas from their original place of burial in Myra to Bari in Apulia, where many Greeks took refuge from the Islamic conquest of Byzantine territories.

December 7
Saint Ambrose,
Bishop and Teacher

Born around A.D. 339 to an aristocratic Christian Roman family in what is now Germany, Ambrose rose in the Roman civil service after his education in Rome. Promoted to the governorship of Milan and its environs, Ambrose established such a good reputation as a fair adminstrator that popular outcry led to his election as bishop of Milan. One complication that stood in the way of Ambrose only briefly was that he was a catechumen at the time of his election. Baptism and ordination to the priesthood and episcopacy followed in swift succession, the last of these sacraments being conferred on December 7, in A.D. 374 Studying theology with a tutor after his episcopal ordination, Ambrose was able to appreciate both Greek and Latin theological traditions. His role as the pastor who baptized Saint Augustine in A.D. 386 has overshadowed his other accomplishments, especially the courage with which he faced up to tyrannical imperial Roman authority in the late fourth century. He died relatively young in A.D. 397 and is especially revered in the local church he once shepherded, Milan.

December 8
Solemnity of the Immaculate Conception of the Blessed Virgin Mary

Readings: Genesis 3:9–15, 20; Ephesians 1:3–6, 11–12; Luke 1:26–38

Protestants are usually dumbfounded by the official name of this feast in Catholic liturgical practice, quite frequently confusing it with the biblical teaching about Mary's virginal conception of Jesus. Not a few Catholics make the same mistake, and the Gospel for this festival, Luke's account of the annunciation, contributes to the problem. A clearer idea of what Catholics celebrate on this day and on the related festival of the Assumption (August 15) can be obtained from Luke's account of how Jesus replied to the listener who blessed him and his mother, making particular mention of her physical relationship to him. The reply of Jesus pointed out the real core of Mary's greatness: not her inimitable mothering of Jesus but her perfect discipleship, that of those "who hear the word of God and observe it" (Lk 11:28).

On the solemnity of the Immaculate Conception of the Virgin Mary we celebrate the triumph of God's grace in this daughter of Israel, the absolute integrity of this purely human being who responded freely and totally to God's terrifying annunciation of her future motherhood: "The holy Spirit will come upon you, and the power of the Most High will over-shadow you. Therefore the child to be born will be called holy, Son of God" (Lk 1:35). For Mary, as Matthew's Gospel empha-sizes, such maternity threatened her with disrepute among her contemporaries and the burdens of single motherhood, to say nothing of suspicion on the part of her fiancé (Mt 1:18–20). Luke's Gospel emphasizes the generosity of this first disciple, even before the birth of the incarnate Servant of Yahweh: "I am the handmaid of the Lord. May it be done to me accord-ing to your word" (Lk 1:38).

The church teaches us that Mary was graced by God from the first moment of her entrance into our history–the moment of her conception in her mother's womb–precisely to make this extraordinary response. Unlike Jesus, whose new humanity, free from the sin of Adam and Eve (narrated in the first reading for this day) burned with the fire of God's august presence, Mary remained only human, but perfectly human: *freed* from sin rather than *free* from sin. The graciousness of God reaches backward and forward in history to give us saints–God's holy ones–before and after the coming of our God in Jesus. From the beginning of human sinfulness God promised eventual victory over the serpent: "I will put enmity between you and the woman,/ and between your offspring and hers;/ He will strike at your head,/ while you strike at his heel" (Gn 3:15). This celebration could as well be called the Predestination of Mary, God's choosing this extraordinary daughter of Abraham to live out to its fullness the vocation of God's Chosen People to holiness. The second reading, from the Epistle to the Ephesians, emphasizes that all of us are so predestined in Christ: "[God] chose us in him, before the foun-dation of the world, to be holy and without blemish before him" (Eph 1:4). Mary has shown us the way to surrender ourselves to that predestination to "praise...his glory, we who first hoped in Christ" (Eph 1:12). The celebration of her Immaculate Conception reminds us that we too must model ourselves on the Servant of Yahweh, whose redemptive death makes possible all holiness in every stage of history.

December 9
Blessed Juan Diego, Visionary and Hermit
(In Mexico, the USA and Elsewhere)

Between the solemnity of the Immaculate Conception and the feast of Our Lady of Guadalupe we remember, in Mexico and neighboring countries in the Americas, another extraordinary miracle of God's graciousness: the almost anonymous sixteenth-century Mexican Indian Juan Diego, the visionary who appropriated the Mother of God for the downtrodden in colonial New Spain. Less than three decades after the arrival of Columbus in the New World and only a decade after the brutal Spanish conquest of the Aztecs, this illiterate Indian peasant recognized in the Virgin of Nazareth a soul mate for himself and for all the colonized and oppressed people of the world. On December 9, 1531, Juan Diego encountered in his vision the Mother of God as an Indian girl very like the woman robed with the sun, standing on the crescent moon and crowned with stars in the Book of Revelation, chapter 12. To the astonishment of the Spanish bishop, Juan Diego presented him some days later with a poncho full of flowers from the Virgin, a poncho which, when opened, revealed a portrait of the girl of Juan Diego's vision. Pope John Paul II beatified Juan Diego.

December 11
Saint Damasus, Pope

An older contemporary of Ambrose of Milan, Damasus–born of a Spanish family residing in Rome–eventually became bishop of Rome at the age of 62 in A.D. 366 and ruled until his death in A.D. 384. Not everything in his prepapal career was exempt from criticism. Ordained a deacon by Pope Liberius, his predecessor, Damasus had backed the antipope Felix II when ecclesiastical push came to shove. When he himself came to succeed Liberius, some of the Roman clergy supported a rival candidate, and violence ensued. Eventually, with the help of the Western Roman Emperor Valentinian II, Damasus established himself in the See of Peter. As bishop of Rome he combated heresy and sponsored Saint Jerome's work of revising the Latin translations of the Old and New Testaments from a close study of the original texts in Hebrew, Aramaic and Greek. Interested in the historical background of the Roman episcopate, Damasus created papal archives and promoted the veneration of the martyrs of Rome's persecuted Christian past.

December 12
Feast of Our Lady
of Guadalupe
(In Mexico, the USA
and Elsewhere)

When they gradually realized how vital a part Hispanic Americans play in the life of the Catholic Church in their country, the bishops of the United States arranged that the solemnity of Our Lady of Guadalupe, celebrated in Mexico and elsewhere, become a feast as well in the whole of the United States. To the present day, not only in Mexico but throughout the world once colonized by Spain, the Virgin of Guadalupe—fondly called *la Morenita* "the little dark-skinned girl"—is the Mother of the oppressed, the poor and the victims of discrimination. Her image is venerated throughout Latin America, the Philippines and wherever Hispanic populations live in the United States. Readings from the common of the Virgin Mary replace those of an ordinary weekday in Advent, but no particular readings are mandated for this feast. The progress within the Advent season from the solemnity of the Immaculate Conception through the memorial of Blessed Juan Diego to the feast of Our Lady of Guadalupe suggests an Advent journey from Palestine to Mexico, from the openness of a perfectly saintly young Jewish woman of the late first century B.C. through the candor of an illiterate Mexican peasant of the early sixteenth century to the woman clothed with the sun coming into her new home wherever the people of her Son gather to celebrate the incarnation of our God in the context of the poor.

Also on December 12
Saint Jane Frances de Chantal, Foundress
(In Canada; in the USA: August 18)

Jeanne Françoise de Chantal–all of whose names come in for usage in France and elsewhere by assorted Janes, Jane Franceses and Chantals–was displaced from December 12 in the United States to give room for Our Lady of Guadalupe, but is undoubtedly beyond feeling any resentment. Born Jeanne Françoise de Fremyot in 1572, she married Baron Christophe de Chantal when she was twenty and gave birth seven times, with four of her children surviving infantile diseases. A widow at the age of twenty-nine (her husband was killed in a shooting accident), Jane determined to live the rest of her life as a celibate. Under the expert spiritual direction of Saint Francis de Sales, Jane Frances determined to found a new and active form of religious life for women, but ecclesiastical worries about the reputation of sisters outside the cloister forced her to envision the Sisters of the Visitation in more conventional terms, at least at first. Enclosure did not keep Jane Frances herself from an active apostolic life, which included the founding of numerous Visitation communities. Through her son, killed fighting the Huguenots in 1627, Jane Frances was the grandmother of the celebrated Parisian epistolary gossip Madame de Sevigne. The grandmother is better remembered as the spiritual friend and confidant of Saint Francis de Sales and Saint Vincent de Paul.

December 13
Saint Lucy, Virgin and Martyr

Before the adjustment of the Julian calendar during the pontificate of Pope Gregory XIII in 1582, the feast of Saint Lucy had come to coincide more or less with the shortest day of the year in the northern hemisphere. John Donne's justly famous "A nocturnall upon Saint Lucies Day, Being the shortest day," written in Protestant London in the early seventeenth century, reflects the fact that England at that time still followed the Julian calendar. Lucy, whose name derives from a Latin word for light (lux, lucis), offers the light of remembered faith and purity and courage on the longest night of the year. To the present day, Swedes begin Saint Lucy's Day being awakened by their youngest daughter wearing a crown of lighted candles and singing a hymn to Saint Lucy while serving a sweet breakfast—not a bad idea on a cold and dark December morning in Sweden. The real Saint Lucy behind these customs is hard to discern beneath the encrustation of later legend. The Roman Canon remembers her as a young female martyr during the persecution of Diocletian, probably in Sicily. Her nominal connection with light and the legend that her persecutors gouged out her eyes (before they were miraculously restored) make her the patroness of those with ophthalmic problems.

December 14
Saint John of the Cross,
Mystical Master

Juan de Yepes, a man short of stature even by the standards of the sixteenth century in which he lived (1542–91), towered over many of his contemporaries in Catholic Spain at its zenith. The brilliance of his poetry and the theological depth of the mystical teaching he imparted in lengthy commentaries on his poetic compositions made him not only a major poet in the Spanish language but also (since 1926) a doctor of the church in matters of the interior life. A disciple of Saint Teresa of Avila at a time when men seldom looked for spiritual guidance from women, John of the Cross—as he came to be known—suffered much at the hands of his fellow Carmelites who opposed the reforms he introduced into the life of the Carmelite friars under the influence of Teresa. Jailed in a Carmelite friary in Toledo under appalling circumstances, John used his time of incarceration fruitfully, elaborating his ascetical and mystical theology of "the dark night of the soul." He managed to escape from the clutches of his brethren and eventually exercised a great influence on the spiritual lives not only of Carmelites, male and female, but on all who seek the inner path to holiness.

"Where have You hidden yourself, my beloved, and left me in tears?" —*John of the Cross,* The Spiritual Canticle

December 21
Saint Peter Canisius,
Priest and Catechist

Peter Canisius (1521–97), born in what is now the Netherlands and educated in what is now Belgium, Latinized his Dutch name (Pieter Kanijs) and lived the rest of his life after 1543 as a pan-European Jesuit, especially in central Europe. There he spearheaded the Counter-Reformation efforts to catechize the vastly ignorant Catholics of what are now Austria, Switzerland, the Czech Republic, Germany and even parts of Italy. Determined to stay free of ecclesiastical administration in one particular place, Canisius (at the urging of his superior general, Saint Ignatius Loyola) turned down an offer to become Archbishop of Vienna. The main technique he used for reeducating Catholics was the question-and-answer style of catechism; so famous was his major contribution to that literary and theological genre that for many years in German-speaking lands people referred to their catechism as their "Canisius." As superior of the Jesuits in Vienna he sent the adolescent Polish aristocrat Saint Stanislaus Kostka on foot to Rome, where, far from his disapproving family, Stanislaus could enter the Jesuit novitiate with the approval of Loyola's second successor as superior general, Saint Francis Borgia.

December 23
Saint John Kanty,
Scholar and Pastor

John of Kanty in Poland (1390–1473) had the misfortune to die on Christmas Eve, but even on the eve of Christmas Eve he gets little attention since his memorial was moved closer to the date of his birth into eternal life from its former positioning on October 20. At a time of less than brilliance in the intellectual life of the Catholic Church, John proved an exception, lecturing in theology at the University of Cracow, although he was forced out of his academic post at one point in his life and appointed, somewhat uncomfortably, to be a parish priest. Eventually recalled to the chair of theology at Cracow, he left behind a reputation not only for learning but also for his concern for the poor and hungry. His academic robes were used after his lifetime to vest newly minted doctors of the university. One cannot help wondering what those more than five-hundred-year-old doctoral robes look like by now.

December 29
Saint Thomas à Becket, Bishop and Martyr

Thomas à Becket (1118–70) was born of Norman parents settled in London not long after the Norman invasion of England in 1066. Poor historical sources available to the twentieth-century French playwright Jean Anouilh led him to present the martyred archbishop in the play *Becket, or The Honor of God* as part of the Anglo-Saxon resistance to the Norman suzerainty, but the historical error did not detract that much from the excitement of Anouilh's play or the subsequent film. T. S. Eliot's verse drama, *Murder in the Cathedral,* more august than Anouilh's version, still comes over as an exciting work on stage. That the struggle between an absolutist king and an archbishop intent on preserving the prerogatives of the church over against government should provide modern theatergoers with two notable plays demonstrates that the focus of medieval England's favorite pilgrimage (witness Chaucer's *Canterbury Tales*) continues to exercise fascination. No saint as a cleric and henchman of Henry II, Becket changed dramatically on becoming archbishop of Canterbury. Conflicts with his erstwhile royal patron drove Thomas into long exile and, after a seeming reconciliation with Henry, finally led to his martyrdom on this date during Christmas week, four weeks after his return to England in December 1170. Henry VIII destroyed the tomb of Thomas à Becket at Canterbury, so much did he hate the memory of an archbishop of Canterbury who had the moral stamina to stand up to absolutist tyranny.

December 31
Saint Sylvester, Pope
and Church-Builder

Sylvester became the bishop of Rome shortly after the Edict of Milan (A.D. 312), in which the newly victorious Constantine gave freedom to the Christian Church. Sylvester lived out his career as pope in relative peace until his death in A.D. 335, and we can be fairly sure that he built the first versions of several of the major churches in the city of Rome, including the Lateran Basilica, the pope's cathedral. Legend has it that Sylvester received the so-called Donation of Constantine (the papal suzerainty over all the other patriarchal churches as well as the governance of much of Italy) from the catechumen emperor, but this idea was first fabricated in the eighth or ninth century A.D. It is unlikely that Sylvester healed Constantine of leprosy or baptized him either, the latter event taking place on Constantine's deathbed two years after Sylvester's own death.

January 2
Saints Basil and Gregory Nazianzen, Theologians and Friends

In some ways it would make more sense to celebrate together the feasts of Saint Basil the Great (A.D. 330–79) and his younger brother Saint Gregory of Nyssa, throwing in for good measure those of another brother, Saint Peter of Sebaste, and their sister, Saint Macrina the Younger, as well as their sainted parents, Basil the Elder and Emmelia, and their grandmother, Saint Macrina the Elder. But that could become tiresome, and the friendship of Basil and Gregory Nazianzen (A.D. 329–89), fellow students in Athens with the man later known as the emperor Julian the Apostate, deserves celebration. Of similar contemplative natures, Basil and Gregory were forced by circumstances into lives of ecclesiastical action, Basil as bishop of Caesarea and Gregory, first as the bishop of Sasima, a dependent diocese in Basil's sphere of influence, as well as coadjutor to his aged father as bishop of Nazianzos and, at a later date, as bishop of Constantinople. Ecclesiastical office led to some disputes between Basil and Gregory, and their friendship cooled but never died off. Gregory wrote brilliantly about the mystery of the Trinity in opposition to Arianism, but Basil, although notable for his theological forays against Arianism (which had imperial support), is better remembered for the monastic rule he formulated, still in use among monks and nuns of the Eastern churches.

January 4
Saint Elizabeth Ann Seton, Widow and Foundress (In the USA)

Elizabeth Bayley Seton (1774–1821), born in New York of prominent Episcopalian parents, married William Seton when she was nineteen, bore him five children, and at twenty-eight, found herself a widow when her husband died while the family was staying in Italy. The kindness of an Italian Catholic family impressed her deeply, and on her return to the United States she became a Catholic herself in 1805. In 1809 she undertook to educate poor Catholic girls in Maryland, with the help of four companions; from this group of lay women emerged the inspiration for the Sisters of Charity of St. Joseph in 1812. Within the next nine years the congregation mushroomed and played a major role in the creation of the Catholic school system in the United States. Although not the first American to be canonized a saint (the immigrant Frances Xavier Cabrini beat her out by twenty-nine years), Seton was the first native-born American to make it to that rank, canonized by Pope Paul VI in 1975.

January 5
Saint John Neumann,
Immigrant and Bishop
(In the USA)

John Neumann (1811–60), born of a German father and a Czech mother, immigrated as a seminarian from his native Bohemia (in the present Czech Republic) to the United States when the anticlerical government of the Austrian empire held up his ordination. The bishop of New York ordained him and sent him to work among German-speaking immigrant Catholics in the area of Buffalo. In 1840, four years after his ordination, Neumann entered the Redemptorist order and excelled in their work of preaching missions up and down the east coast of the United States. After some time as a pastor in Baltimore, Neumann was appointed bishop of Philadelphia in 1852. Over the next eight years Neumann built churches and schools in Philadelphia and its environs with incredible energy, working himself to death in the process. The Catholics of Philadelphia did not forget their tireless bishop, and in 1977 he was finally canonized by Pope Paul VI.

January 6
Blessed André Bessette, Worker
(In Canada and the USA)

Brother André Bessette (1845–1937), a Holy Cross brother from French Canada, had worked for a time in a hat factory in Danbury, Connecticut, before he entered the Congregation of the Holy Cross in Canada at the age of twenty-five. For the next sixty-seven years, in and around Montreal, he held the most ordinary of jobs as a brother–janitor, gardener, infirmarian– taking Saint Joseph as his model. Eventually his reputation for holiness spread and people sought his prayer in times of sickness; he usually asked the intercession of Saint Joseph in all such petitions to God. Fifty-five years after his death he was beatified by Pope John Paul II.

January 7
Saint Raymond of Penyafort, Canonist

Raymond of Penyafort (1180?–1275), a Spanish-Catalan civil and canon lawyer, entered the Order of Preachers (Dominican friars) when he was already over forty years of age, one year after the death of Saint Dominic. He participated fully in the revival of sacred learning that typified the work of the first generation of Dominicans, cooperating in the task of compiling canon law initiated by Pope Gregory IX. Reluctant to take on leadership positions in the church or the Dominican order, Raymond served for only two years as master general of the Dominicans, during which time he revised their constitutions. He then resigned and returned to Spain, where he wrote to encourage his younger contemporary, Thomas Aquinas, to write the *Summa contra Gentiles*.

January 13
Saint Hilary of Poitiers, Theologian

Just about the last saint to be able to make an appearance in the cycle of Advent, Christmas and Epiphany is a theologian with a pleasant name derived from the Latin *hilaris,* meaning not "hilarious," but "cheerful." Both men (e.g., Hilaire Belloc) and women (e.g., Hillary Rodham Clinton) bear variants of his name. His feast day lends its name to the second term at Oxford and some other universities of British heritage because it marks the end of the Christmas holiday. Born around A.D. 315 to pagan parents, Hilary only became a Christian in A.D. 350 and was elected bishop of Poitiers a scant three years later. Like Ambrose, Basil and Gregory Nazianzen, his younger contemporaries, Hilary spent much of his energy expounding orthodox theology against the Arians, who had garnered imperial support for their demotion of Jesus from the status of equality with God. His courage in defending the truth of God incarnate brought him temporary banishment from his diocese in the south of France by the Arian emperor Constantius. Hilary died back in Poitiers in approximately A.D. 368.